vSphere Design Pocketbook 2.0 Blog Edition

Full-Sized Design Considerations

for your Software-Defined Data Center

vSphere Design Pocketbook 2.0 – Blog Edition ©2014 by PernixData.

All rights reserved. No part of this publication may be reproduced, distributed, or transmitted in any form or by any means, including photocopying, recording, or other electronic or mechanical methods, without the prior written permission of the publisher, except in the case of brief quotations embodied in critical reviews and certain other noncommercial uses permitted by copyright law.

All terms mentioned in this book that are known to be trademarks or service marks have been appropriately capitalized.

Use of a term in this book should not be regarded as affecting the validity of any trademark or service mark.

Contents

Chapter 1 – Host Configuration

Percentage Based Admission Control Gives Lower
VM Restart Guarantee? – Duncan Epping 1-2

VMware Slot Sizes – Eric Shanks 1-7

VMware vSphere Misidentifies Local or SAN-attached
SSD Drives as Non-SSD – Yury Magalif 1-12

Chapter 2 – Cluster and vCenter Design

vSphere Island Clusters – Dee Abson 2-2

Adding a Secondary NIC to the vCenter 5.1
Appliance (VCSA) – Christian Mohn 2-8

vCenter Design – Abdullah Abdullah 2-11

Designing a VMware 5.5 Management
Cluster – Michael Wilmsen 2-16

Chapter 3 – Storage Configuration

Thin Provisioning Considerations When Formatting
Volumes in a Guest OS – Cormac Hogan 3-2

Host Isolation Response Configuration for
IP Storage – Josh Odgers 3-9

The Parent Virtual Disk Has Been Modified
Since the Child was Created – Patrick Kremer 3-12

Chapter 4 – Network and Security Design

What is Network Virtualization? – Brad Hedlund	4-2
Potential Network Black Hole Issue – David Pasek	4-9
Enable NIOC (Network I/O Control) on All your Distributed Switches, Wherever Possible – Ather Beg	4-17
Designing Redundancy: Designing for Failure - Peter Chang	4-20

Chapter 5 – VM Configuration

Considerations When Migrating VMs Between vCenter Servers – William Lam	5-2
VMware vSphere 5.5 Virtual Storage Adapter Performance – Michael Webster	5-8
Design considerations for Virtual Machine Time Synchronization – Aylin Sali	5-11

Chapter 6 – Application Landscape

Words of Wisdom...Exchange Virtualization and the Storage Behind It – Phoummala Schmitt	6-2
Impact of Write Acceleration on Your Backups – Tom Queen	6-8

Chapter 7 – Words of Wisdom

vSphere Web Client Short Cuts – Cormac Hogan	7-2
Systems Thinking Impacting Design Decisions – Todd Mace	7-3
IT Infrastructure Design – Martijn Baecke	7-6

Foreword

The VMware community is a special one. In my many years of IT, I have not seen a more active, passionate, and engaged group of people.

The amount of time and effort people invest in supporting and building the VMware community is astonishing, with amazing initiatives every day like VCAP and VCDX study groups, podcasts, vbrownbag webinars, vBeers, and unique challenges like the one offered by the team of virtualdesignmaster.com.

Because the VMware community loves to share advice, in 2013 I created the vSphere Design Pocketbook 1.0. Experts were challenged to create very focused messages that were no longer than a single tweet (i.e. 140 characters). The book ended up being a tremendous hit, with PernixData distributing over 10,000 copies!

This year, I wanted to give a bigger canvas to contributors, allowing them to submit recommendations, hints, and tips without the character limit. In essence, I wanted to tap into the blogosphere and re-purpose as much of the great content as possible.

Many of you were eager to submit. To that end, I received lots of great content, and I want to thank everyone who participated. But, in the spirit of creating a manageable sized "pocketbook", we could not publish everything. Some tough choices had to be made.

Below is the final result. I am pleased to introduce the vSphere PocketBook 2.0 – Blog Edition. It showcases some of the best articles from the virtualization community over the past year, covering everything from new technology introductions to highly detailed vm configuration recommendations and IT infrastructure design considerations. This was an extremely fun project for me, which I feel underscores some of the best aspects of the VMware community. I hope you enjoy the results.

If you happen to be at VMworld, VMUGs, or any other event where you bump into community members who have provided you valuable content, I encourage you to talk to them and tell them you like their work. A little appreciation goes a long way – and it's the fuel that keeps these amazing people going.

Frank Denneman
Technology Evangelist, PernixData

Twitter: @FrankDenneman

Blog: frankdenneman.nl

Chapter 1 – Host Configuration

Percentage Based Admission Control Gives Lower VM Restart Guarantee?

Those who have configured vSphere HA have all seen that section where it asks if you want to use admission control or not. Of course if you decide you want to use it, and you should want this, then the next question that comes is which one do you want to use? I have always preferred the "Percentage Based Admission Control" policy. For some reason though there are people who think that the percentage based admission control policy rules out large VMs from being restarted or offers a lower guarantee.

The main perception that people have is that the percentages based admission control policy gives lower guarantees of virtual machines being restarted than the "host failures" admission control policy. So let break it down, and I mean BREAK IT DOWN, by using an example.

Example:

- 5 hosts
- 200 GB of Memory in cluster
- 20 GHz of CPU in cluster

If **no reservations** are set:

Percentage Based will do the following:

1. The Percentage Based policy will take the total amount of resources and subtract the amount of resources reserved for fail-over. If that percentage is for instance 20% than 40GB and 4GHz are subtracted. Which means 160GB and 16GHz are left.

2. The reserved resources for every virtual machine that is powered on is subtracted from what the outcome of 1 was. If no reservation is set memory then memory overhead is

subtracted, if the memory overhead is 200MB then 200MB is subtracted from the 160GB that was left resulting in 159.8GB being available. For CPU the default of 32MHz will be used.

3. You can power-on virtual machines until the amount of available resources, according to HA Admission Control, is depleted, yes many VMs in this case.

Host Failures will do the following:

1. The Host Failures policy will calculate the amount of slots. A slot is formed out of two components: memory and CPU. As no reservation is used the default for CPU is used which is 32MHz, with vSphere 5.0 and higher. For memory the largest memory overhead size is used, in this scenario there could be a variety of sizes lets say the smallest is 64MB and the largest 300MB. Now 300MB will be used for the Memory Slot size.

2. Now that the slot size is known Admission Control will look for the host with the most slots (available resources / slot size) and subtract those slots from the total amount of available slots. (If one host failure is specified). Every time a VM is started a slot is subtracted. If a VM is started with a higher memory reservation we go back to 1 and the math will need to be done again.

3. You can power-on virtual machines until you are out of slots, again... many VMs.

If **reservations are set**:

Percentage Based will do the following:

1. The Percentage Based policy will take the total amount of resources and subtract the amount of resources reserved for fail-over. If that percentage is for instance 20% than 40GB and 4GHz are subtracted. Which means 160GB and 16GHz are left.
2. The reserved resources for every virtual machine that is powered on is subtracted from what the outcome of 1 was. So if 10GB of memory was reserved, then 10GB is subtracted resulting in 150GB being available.
3. You can power-on virtual machines until available resources are depleted (according to HA Admission Control), but as reservations are used you are "limited" in terms of the amount of VMs you can power-on.

Host Failures will do the following:

1. The Host Failures policy will calculate the amount of slots. A slot is formed out of two components: memory and CPU. As a reservation is used for memory but not for CPU the default for CPU is used which is 32MHz, with vSphere 5.0 and higher. For memory there is a 10GB reservation set. 10GB will be used for the Memory Slot size.
2. Now that the slot size is known Admission Control will look for the host with the most slots (available resources / slot size) and subtract those slots from the total amount of available slots. (If one host failure is specified). Every time a VM is started a slot is subtracted, yes that is a 10GB memory slot, even if it has for instance a 2GB reservation. If a VM is started with a higher memory reservation we go back to 1 and the math will need to be done again.

3. You can power-on virtual machines until you are out of slots, as a high reservation is set you will be severely limited!

Now you can imagine that "Host Failures" can be on the safe side... If you have 1 reservation set the math will be done with that reservation. This means that a single 10GB reservation **will impact** how many VMs you can power-on until HA screams that it is out of resources. But at least you are guaranteed you can power them on right? Well yes, but realistically speaking people disable Admission Control at this point as that single 10GB reservation allows you to power on just a couple of VMs. (16 to be precise.)

But that beats Percentage Based right... because if I have a lot of VMs who says my VM with 10GB reservation can be restarted? First of all, if there are no "unreserved resources" available on any given host to start this virtual machine then vSphere HA will ask vSphere DRS to defragment the cluster. As HA Admission Control had already accepted this virtual machine to begin with, chances are fairly high that DRS can solve the fragmentation.

Also, as the percentage based admission control policy uses reservations AND memory overhead... how many virtual machines do you need to have powered-on before your VM with 10 GB memory reservation is denied to be powered-on? It would mean that **none of the hosts** has 10GB of unreserved memory available. That is not very likely as that means you would need to power-on hundreds of VMs... Probably way too many for your environment to ever perform properly. So chances of hitting this scenario are limited, extremely small.

Conclusion

Although theoretically possible, it is very unlikely you will end up in situation where one or multiple virtual machines can not be restarted when using the Percentage Based Admission Control policy. Even if you are using reservations on all virtual machines then this is unlikely as the virtual machines have been accepted at some point by HA Admission Control and HA will leverage DRS to defragment resources at that point. Also keep in mind that when using reservations on all virtual machines that Host Failures is not an option as it will skew your numbers as it does the math with "worst case scenario", a single 10GB reservation can kill your ROI/TCO.

About the Author

Duncan Epping is a Chief Technologist working for VMware. Duncan specializes in software-defined storage, hyper-converged platforms, and availability solutions. Duncan was among the first VMware Certified Design Experts (VCDX 007). Duncan is the owner of Yellow-Bricks.com and author of various books including Essential Virtual SAN and the Clustering Deepdive series. You can follow him on twitter @DuncanYB.

VMware Slot Sizes

VMware slot sizes are an important topic if you're concerned with how many ESXi hosts are required to run your environment.

What is a Slot?

A slot is the minimum amount of CPU and memory resources required for a single VM in an ESXi cluster. Slot size is an important concept because it affects admission control.

A VMware ESXi cluster needs a way to determine how many resources need to be available in the event of a host failure. This slot calculation gives the cluster a way to reserve the right amount of resources.

How are Slots Sized?

The slot has two parts, the CPU component and the memory component. Each of them has its own calculation. If there are no virtual machine resource reservations in the cluster, then the slot size (for ESXi 5 at least) is 32 MHz for CPU and 0 MBs + overhead for memory. (I've used 80 MBs as my memory overhead in the examples)

On to an incredibly simplistic diagram...

In the example below we have 2 ESXi hosts that have the same amount of resources available for virtual machines. There are different sized VMs, but none of them have a reservation. Doing a quick calculation we can determine that 384 slots are available on each host.

CPU Component: 4 X 3.0 GHz / 2000 MHz = 384 slots

Memory Component: 49 GBs / 4024 MBs = 627 slots

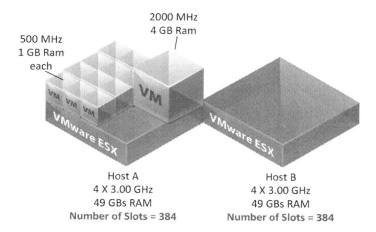

SLOT SIZE =
CPU – 32 MHz
Memory - ~80 MB

2000 MHz
4 GB Ram

500 MHz
1 GB Ram
each

Host A
4 X 3.00 GHz
49 GBs RAM
Number of Slots = 384

Host B
4 X 3.00 GHz
49 GBs RAM
Number of Slots = 384

We take the lower value between the CPU slot size and the memory slot size to determine the number of virtual machines that can be started up under admission control. So therefore, we could safely start 384 machines on these ESXi hosts, have one fail, and have the other host start all of them.

(I should mention that it's unlikely that you could get 384 vms on one of these hosts. That would be a great consolidation ratio.)

Problem Scenario

What if you have a single large VM with a reservation, but the rest of the virtual machines are relatively small?

Let's look at the same environment, but this time let's make the larger VM have a reservation on it.

CPU Component: 4 X 3.0 GHz / 2000 MHz = 6 slots

Memory Component: 49 GBs / 4024 MBs = 12 slots

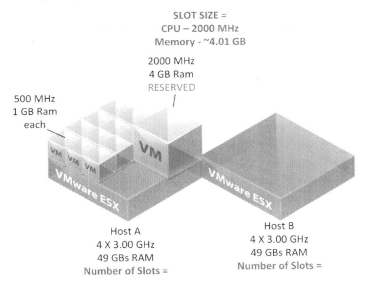

Admission control is going to tell us that only 6 slots are available on host B, so it will only allow 6 VMs on host A to be powered on. Since I'm using a simplistic diagram with only two hosts, we know that these VMs will still fit on the host but since we use the largest slot size to determine how much we can fail over admission control will stop us from powering on VMs.

What are our options?

Option 1 – Don't use reservations unless there is a good reason to do so.

Option 2 – We can manually configure the slot size on the cluster.

Navigate to the cluster settings and go to the HA Section, Click Edit and you'll have the option of modifying the slot size. Note that if you do this, some of your VMs will require multiple slots to run. For instance the large VM we used in our example might take more than 1 slot depending on what size you make it. The button below the slot size configuration may help you determine how many VMs will be affected by this change.

☑ Enable Host Monitoring

Admission control is a policy used by vSphere HA to ensure failover capacity within a cluster. Raising the proportion of ensured host failures increases the availability constraints and capacity reserved in the cluster.

◉ Define failover capacity by static number of hosts.

　　Reserved failover capacity: [1] Hosts

　　Slot size policy:
　　　　○ Cover all powered-on virtual machines
　　　　　　Calculate slot size based on the maximum CPU/Memory reservation and overhead of all powered-on virtual machines.
　　　　◉ Fixed slot size
　　　　　　Specify the slot size explicitly.
　　　　　　CPU slot size: [32] MHz
　　　　　　Memory slot size: [79] MB

　　VMs requiring multiple slots: View   [Calculate]

View Your Slot Size

If you're curious about what the slot size is on your system, look at your cluster summary. There will be an item listed for slot size.

Summary

If you're in a situation where you think you need to add extra ESXi hosts to your cluster because you can't power on virtual machines without exceeding your admission control rules, take a look at your slot sizes first. It may save you some money on a host you don't really need.

About the Author

Eric Shanks is the principle of theITHollow.com which is a blog focusing on how and why technologies are used in the data center. His background covers a variety of technologies including networking, storage, servers and of course VMware technologies. Over his career he has spent time as a System Engineer and later as Vice President of a consulting company in Chicago. He has earned the industry distinction of vExpert for two years running as well as being a PernixPro. His certifications include VCAP5-DCA\DCD, CCNA, MCITP and others. During his spare time, he also volunteers as a VMUG Leader in Chicago.

VMware vSphere Misidentifies Local or SAN-attached SSD Drives as Non-SSD

Editors Note: Although the steps listed here are required for VMware vSphere Flash Read Cache and the resulting configuration is compatible, they are not required by PernixData FVP™. FVP seamlessly operates with all host flash devices by default, regardless of how they are identified by ESXi.

When sizing and scaling your environment take into consideration using local SSD drives for host local caching solutions like vFlash Read Cache and PernixData.

However, a common problem that arises with Host Cache is the inability of vSphere to recognize all SSD drives as SSD. If the drive type is NOT SSD, Host Cache Configuration will not be allowed. Thus, the following solution is necessary for remediation.

Solution:

Apply some CLI commands to force ESXi into understanding that your drive is really SSD. Then reconfigure your Host Cache.

Instructions:

Look up the name of the disk and its naa.xxxxxx number in VMware GUI. In another example, we found that the disks that are not properly showing as SSD are:

- Dell Serial Attached SCSI Disk (naa.600508e0000000002ed-c6d0e4e3bae0e) — local SSD

- DGC Fibre Channel Disk (naa.60060160a89128005a6304b-3d121e111) — SAN-attached SSD

Check in the GUI that both show up as non-SSD type.

SSH to ESXi host. Each ESXi host will require you to look up the unique disk names and perform the commands below separately, once per host.

Type the following commands, and find the NAA numbers of your disks.

In the examples below, the relevant information is highlighted in GRAY.

The commands you need to type are BOLD.

The comments on commands are in *ITALICS*.

~ # **esxcli storage nmp device list**

naa.600508e0000000002edc6d0e4e3bae0e

Device Display Name: Dell Serial Attached SCSI Disk (naa.600508e0000000002edc6d0e4e3bae0e)

Storage Array Type: VMW_SATP_LOCAL

Storage Array Type Device Config: SATP VMW_SATP_LOCAL does not support device configuration.

Output omitted for space considerations

Device Display Name: DGC Fibre Channel Disk (naa.60060160a89128005a6304b3d121e111)

Storage Array Type: VMW_SATP_ALUA_CX

Storage Array Type Device Config: {navireg=on, ipfilter=on}{implicit_support=on;explicit_support=on; explicit_allow=on;alua_followover=on;{TPG_id=1,TPG_state=ANO}{TPG_id=2,TPG_state=AO}}

Output omitted for space considerations

Host Configuration | 1-13

Note that the Storage Array Type is VMW_SATP_LOCAL for the local SSD drive and VMW_SATP_ALUA_CX for the SAN-attached SSD drive.

Now we will check to see if in CLI, ESXi reports the disks as SSD or non-SSD for both disks. Make sure to specify your own NAA number when typing the command.

~ # esxcli storage core device list
–device=naa.**600508e0000000002edc6d0e4e3bae0e**

naa.600508e0000000002edc6d0e4e3bae0e

Display Name: Dell Serial Attached SCSI Disk (naa.600508e0000000002edc6d0e4e3bae0e)

Is SSD: false

> Output omitted for space considerations

~ # esxcli storage core device list
–device=naa.**60060160a89128005a6304b3d121e111**

naa.60060160a89128005a6304b3d121e111

Display Name: DGC Fibre Channel Disk (naa.60060160a89128005a6304b3d121e111)

Is SSD: false

Output omitted for space considerations

Now we will add a rule to enable SSD on those 2 disks. Make sure to specify your own NAA number when typing the commands.

~ # esxcli storage nmp satp rule add –satp VMW_SATP_LOCAL –device naa.600508e0000000002edc6d0e4e3bae0e –option=enable_ssd

~ # esxcli storage nmp satp rule add –satp VMW_SATP_ALUA_CX –device naa.60060160a89128005a6304b3d121e111 –option=enable_ssd

---

Next, we will check to see that the commands took effect for the 2 disks.

~ # esxcli storage nmp satp rule list | grep enable_ssd

VMW_SATP_ALUA_CX   naa.60060160a89128005a6304b-3d121e111   enable_ssd   user

VMW_SATP_LOCAL   naa.600508e0000000002edc6d0e4e-3bae0e   enable_ssd   user

---

Then, we will run storage reclaim commands on those 2 disks. Make sure to specify your own NAA number when typing the commands.

~ # esxcli storage core claiming reclaim -d naa.60060160a89128005a6304b3d121e111

~ # esxcli storage core claiming reclaim -d naa.600508e0000000002edc6d0e4e3bae0e

Unable to unclaim path vmhba0:C1:T0:L0 on device naa.600508e0000000002edc6d0e4e3bae0e. Some paths may be left in an unclaimed state. You will need to claim them manually using the appropriate commands or wait for periodic path claiming to reclaim them automatically.

If you get the error message above, that's OK. It takes time for the reclaim command to work.

You can check in the CLI by running the command below and looking for "Is SSD: false"

~ # esxcli storage core device list —device=naa.600508e0000000002edc6d0e4e3bae0e

naa.600508e0000000002edc6d0e4e3bae0e

Display Name: Dell Serial Attached SCSI Disk (naa.600508e0000000002edc6d0e4e3bae0e)

Is SSD: false

        Output omitted for space considerations

Check in the vSphere Client GUI. Rescan storage. If it still does NOT say SSD, reboot the ESXi host. Then look in the GUI and rerun the command below.

~ # esxcli storage core device list —device=naa.60060160a89128005a6304b3d121e111

naa.60060160a89128005a6304b3d121e111

Display Name: DGC Fibre Channel Disk (naa.60060160a89128005a6304b3d121e111)

Is SSD: true

        Output omitted for space considerations

If it still does NOT say SSD, you need to wait. Eventually, the command works and displays as SSD in CLI and the GUI.

View: Datastores Devices								
Devices							Refresh	Resc
Name	Runtime Name	Operational State	LUN	Type	Drive Type	Transport	Capacity	Owner
Local LSI Disk (naa.600605b003c5...	vmhba2:C2:T1:L0	Mounted	0	disk	Non-SSD	Parallel SCSI	1.63 TB	NMP
Local LSI Disk (naa.600605b003c5...	vmhba2:C2:T0:L0	Mounted	0	disk	SSD	Parallel SCSI	135.97 G	NMP
Local ATA Disk (t10.ATA____EMC...	vmhba3:C0:T0:L0	Mounted	0	disk	SSD	Parallel SCSI	326.04 G	NMP

About the Author

Yury Magalif is a VDI, Cloud & Virtualization Architect that lives & breathes new Data Center, Storage tech. Worked for Fortune 500, presentations in Top 10 at HP Discover conferences. Principal Architect at CDI in Teterboro, NJ and vExpert 2014.

Twitter: @YuryMagalif
Blog: cloud-zebra.com
okzebra@gmail.com

Chapter 2 –
Cluster and vCenter Design

vSphere Island Clusters

Sit Right Back and You'll Hear a Tale

A very important, and sometimes under appreciated, area of vSphere design is the humble cluster. The cluster is a fairly well understood concept. After all, it's just a grouping of ESXi hosts, right? Well, yes, however you need to consider carefully the types of clusters that will satisfy your design requirements.

Most vSphere designers understand that there are good reasons to separate production from non-production (i.e. development or prototyping) workloads. It follows then that a Production and Non-production cluster meet these needs by restricting these workloads to their appropriate group of hosts. It has also become quite common to dedicate a cluster to Management workloads.

Management workloads typically include vCenter Server, vCenter Operations Manager, Active Directory, DNS, DHCP, etc. Basically any workloads that support infrastructure and whose interruption would cause issues for workloads responsible for business services. Separating these types of workloads allows for various benefits:

- Explicit separation of maintenance windows so that Management workloads remain available while workloads in other clusters are being addressed.

- Ability to have very clear separation of roles and duties in order to ensure that only those administrators with the proper authorization can attend to the Management workloads.

- Resource isolation to ensure that any resource contention among business service workloads doesn't impact Management workloads, as that would in turn affect all workloads.

If our cluster design were to follow these guidelines, then we might now have a collection of clusters that resembles the diagram below.

This cluster design should satisfy the majority of your workload requirements. Infrastructure and management workloads are placed in the *Management Cluster*, development and test workloads in the *Non-Production Cluster*, and all production workloads in the *Production Cluster*. But how to you handle a set of outlier workloads? Workloads that, due to various reasons, shouldn't or can't belong to one of these standard clusters?

The Weather Started Getting Rough

The term Island Cluster was coined within the VMware architecture and design community. It represents any separate vSphere cluster created to support workloads that need to be segregated from the existing clusters. Island Clusters are typically smaller in size as they are purpose built and likely have a limited number of VMs.

As a rule of thumb you want to make sure that your workloads belong to the established clusters within your design, in order to take full advantage of the benefits clusters provide. Segregating workloads into an Island Cluster isn't a light decision to make and should be treated as an exception to the clustering rule.

So what situations or criteria could provide enough justification for you to consider an Island Cluster?

- Strict security requirements that necessitate an enhanced separation between workloads. For example some organizations will not tolerate DMZ and production workloads co-existing on the same host or cluster.

- King of Monster VMs may need to rule their own island. Extremely resource intensive workloads may perform best, and impact other workloads the least, if isolated on their own cluster. This could be especially true if there are significant vCPU allocation variations among your workloads. Make sure that your performance testing bears this out before considering it.

- Licensing, which is the most common reason to consider Island Clusters. You may want to constrain OS licensing by building clusters dedicated to particular platforms, such as one cluster for Windows Server and another for your favourite licensed Linux distribution. Application licensing constraints tied to server resources are a favourite.

The keen reader has likely already figured out that the *Management Cluster* mentioned earlier is a type of Island Cluster. In that case a separate cluster was created for both resource and security reasons. If those reasons didn't exist, then those workloads would be placed in the *Production Cluster* along with the other production workloads.

Now that we have an idea of the types of things to consider when deciding to design an Island Cluster, how do we determine what that cluster should look like?

This Uncharted Desert Isle

As we discussed earlier, Island Clusters are typically purpose built and smaller in size than your traditional clusters. Expect most clusters to contain only two or three hosts. Of course all clusters need at least two hosts, however if you require high availability for your workloads, even during scheduled maintenance, then it's recommended that you dedicate at least three. That way you can have two hosts running while you perform maintenance on the third. Otherwise, follow the same guidelines that you normally use when sizing a cluster.

One consideration that may make your Island Cluster hosts look different from the rest is if you need to constrain physical resources. Why would you do this? Most often in response to licensing constraints. Some application vendors tie their licenses to hardware resources. In these cases if we don't consider an Island Cluster then we may be spending much more than necessary. Let's use Oracle as a working example.

Oracle licensing is notorious for tying licenses to the total number of CPUs available on the server hardware. In the case of a vSphere cluster, that would mean having to count every core of every processor on every host within the cluster. There is then a CPU multiplier value that Oracle supplies that you have to take into account.

Let's assume that within your design you have to make sure that you can virtualize the four existing Oracle database servers. For the purpose of simplicity, they're all standalone, RAC is not in use. Each server currently has two Intel four core processors. Our current Production Cluster has four hosts with two Intel eight core processors.

Okay, so our Production Cluster exceeds the system requirements of the Oracle database servers. Option one is to virtualize the Oracle servers and place them in the Production Cluster. No resource constraints and no security concerns. What does this mean for our licensing?

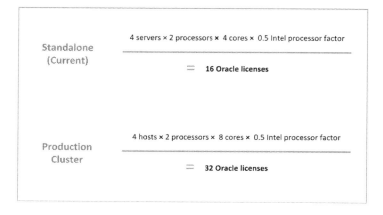

Turns out that simply virtualizing our existing Oracle database servers into our current Production cluster doubles the licenses we require. Now what if we were to consider building a dedicated Island Cluster. Let's call it the *Oracle Cluster*. We'll select two hosts with two Intel six core processors. What would our licensing look like then?

```
Oracle        2 hosts × 2 processors × 6 cores × 0.5 Intel processor factor
Cluster       ─────────────────────────────────────────────────────────────
                              = 12 Oracle licenses
```

Subject to some performance testing to verify that our Oracle database workload needs are being met, we've just reduced our Oracle database licenses and potentially justified the use of an Island Cluster.

The specifics of this example are, of course, hypothetical. They do illustrate the fact though, that through careful consideration and diligence in measuring against our requirements, Island Clusters have a place in our designs.

A Three Hour Tour

In summary, Island Clusters can address the outlier workloads that don't fit into your standard cluster design model. They can save you grief or relieve some pressure on your company's purse strings. They should, however, always be considered very carefully and treated as a design exception. You need to make sure that your VMs behave like happy holidayers on their island and not forgotten castaways.

About the Author

Dee Abson is a technical architect from Alberta, Canada. He's been working with technology for over 20 years and specializes in server and virtualization infrastructure. Working with VMware products since ESX 2 he holds several VMware certifications including the VCP5-DCV. He blogs at http://teebeedee.org and you can connect with him on Twitter @deeabson.

Adding A Secondary NIC to the vCenter 5.1 Appliance (VCSA)

While building my lab environment, I ran into a situation where I wanted to have a completely sealed off networking segment that had no outside access.

This is a trivial task on it's own, just create a vSwitch with no physical NICs attached to it, and then connect the VMs to it. The VMs will then have interconnectivity, but no outside network access at all.

In this particular case, I was setting up a couple of nested ESXi servers that I wanted to connect to the "outside" vCenter Appliance (VCSA). This VCSA instance was not connected to the internal-only vSwitch, but rather to the existing vSwitch that as local network access.

Naturally, the solution would be to add a secondary NIC to the VCSA, and connect that to the internal-only vSwitch.

It turns out that adding a secondary NIC to a VCSA instance, isn't as straight-forward as you might think.

Sure, adding a new NIC is no problem through either the vSphere Client, or the vSphere Web Client, but getting the NIC configured inside of VCSA is another matter.

If you add a secondary NIC, it will turn up in the VCSA management web page, but you will not be able to save the configuration since the required configuration files for eth1 is missing.

In order to rectify this, I performed the following steps:

1. Connect to the VCSA via SSH (default username and password is root/vmware)

2. Copy /etc/sysconfig/networking/devices/ifcfg-eth0 to /etc/sysconfig/networking/devices/ifcfg-eth1

3. Edit ifcfg-eth1 and replace the networking information with your values, here is how mine looks:
   DEVICE=eth1
   BOOTPROTO='static'
   STARTMODE='auto'
   TYPE=Ethernet
   USERCONTROL='no'
   IPADDR='172.16.1.52'
   NETMASK='255.255.255.0'
   BROADCAST='172.16.1.255'

4. Create a symlink for this file in /etc/sysconfig/network
   ln -s /etc/sysconfig/networking/devices/ifcfg-eth1 /etc/sysconfig/network/ifcfg-eth1

5. Restart the networking service to activate the new setup:
   service network restart
   Check the VCSA web management interface to verify that the new settings are active

Cluster and vCenter Design | 2-9

By adding a secondary NIC, configuring it and connecting it to the isolated vSwitch I was now able to add my sequestered nested ESXi hosts to my existing VCSA installation.

There may be several reasons for a setup like this, perhaps you want your VCSA to be available on a management VLAN but reach ESXi hosts on another VLAN without having routing in place between the segmented networks, or you just want to play around with it like I am in this lab environment.

Disclaimer:

Is this supported by VMware? Probably not, but I simply don't know. Caveat emptor, and all that jazz.

About the Author

Christian Mohn is a four-time VMware vExpert (2011/2012/2013/2014), an IT industry veteran, author, podcaster and blogger with more than 17 years of experience. He currently works as a Virtualization Architect for Norway's largest IT company EVRY, where he designs and implements virtualization solutions for enterprise clients as well as serving as the Tech Champion for server virtualization.

Blog: http://vNinja.net - Twitter: @h0bbel

vCenter Design

A lot of debate exists when designing a vCenter Server, whether to place it as a virtual machine, or build a physical server for it the decision varies with the variety of the enterprises out there as each entity has its own needs and its own requirement.

And here goes....

Scenario [1] (vCenter + Hosts):

You have a 2 to N number of ESXi hosts that you need to manage with no dependency on the vCenter Server services other than management, here it'll do just fine to virtual the vCenter Server as HA will take care of any host failure and will vMotion the vCenter Server virtual machine to another host with an acceptable downtime as the production environment will still function and you'll get your precious management access to the vCenter Server within the next couple of minutes or in case of extreme cases you'd rebuild it and restore the database from a backup (you do have backups? No ;-)?).

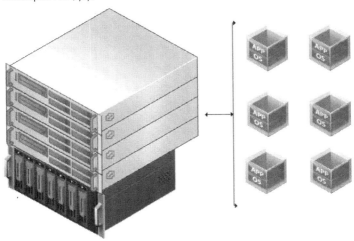

Scenario [2] (vCenter + Hosts) + Horizon View / + SRM / + Any other product with vCenter Server dependency:

Here we've introduced a new dependency which is other products that require the vCenter Server to be up and running to able to function correctly.

For example if you're going to use the Composer line of provisioning then for sure the vCenter Server here becomes something very critical and in case it goes down then you won't be able to have the control you need over the virtual desktop infrastructure.

Another example would be utilizing SRM for replicating your virtual machines, and performing failover and failback operations, losing the vCenter Server would mean losing the SRM connection to all underlying components.

Also a good example would be backups, as all backup software now rely on the vCenter Server to get them into underlying infrastructure so without vCenter you won't have virtual machine backups.

So here we start thinking of ways to protect the vCenter Server against downtime, taking into consideration:

1. Host failure: here definitely HA will kick in and the day will be saved.

2. VM failure: well this is rare but can happen never the less, bad backups causing bad snapshots or maybe an administrator fiddling here and so on and so forth.

3. OS failure (residing on a virtual of physical machine): It's just never safe enough with Windows, really I do like the operating system but the tendency for it to break randomly is a fact that can't be neglected.

Solutions?

So what to do?

Supported by VMware:

1. We used to have vCenter Server Heartbeat but its end of availability was announced in June 2014 and sadly there is no replacement for it yet, on the other hand you can still but a suite from Neverfail (this is what vCenter Server Heartbeat was based on) where they have something call IT continuity suite but I am sure it will cost a fortune.

2. You can use vSphere Replication to replicate the vCenter Server to a local host but this is not real time high availability and you must power on the vCenter Server manually, you may also use any other supported replication software for that matter.

3. You can schedule a PowerCLI script to clone the vCenter Server virtual machine on a daily basis.

4. Rely on backups in case of disaster to restore the whole virtual machine.

Unsupported by VMware:

Finally you can go with the unsupported way, something I that I have been working on lately based on Windows Server 2012 Failover Cluster Manager, here is a diagram that would explain the idea behind this solution:

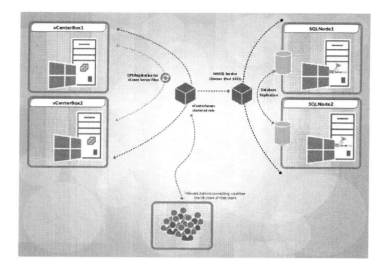

The above diagram suggests utilizing Microsoft's Failover Cluster Manager to create a role based cluster to make the vCenter Server services high available on two nodes and above, it works perfectly along with other products but with one down side which is that each time you perform a change on the primary node you must failover to the secondary node so that the registry changes would replicate, other than that it works.

Thank you for taking the time to read this.

About the Author

Abdullah Abdullah lives and works in Beirut - Lebanon He is a Senior Support Specialist with experience in IT solutions integration especially in VMware, Microsoft, Citrix, Symantec and Veeam products along with an extensive experience in HP enterprise portfolio.

Hobbies: Reading, Hacking games, testing new products in lab and taking part of BETA programs, hacking games, swimming, diving and consuming sugary stuff #SayNoToDiet.

Blog: http://notes.doodzzz.net

Twitter: @do0dzZZ

Designing a VMware 5.5 Management Cluster

In the past we had our vCenter server on his own physical machine. Later we moved vCenter to a virtual machine on the same cluster where all other virtual machine live.

As we get more, bigger and more VMware techniques in our VMware environments, the need for a separate vSphere cluster for VMware services is growing so we can guarantee that the base for our VMware environment isn't affected by resource consumption of other (production) virtual machines and of course the same applies the other way around.

A separate VMware management cluster has the following benefits:

- Separate management resource from production resources.

- The management services don't run on the same hardware as your production environment.

- In case of a complete power-down situation, you first start your management cluster with all VMware services. If all VMware services are up and running you can start the VMware clusters for your production environment making sure that everything you need for a controlled power-up of you production services is in order.

- Ability to reboot a virtual machine without effecting other VMware services.

There are several VMware vSphere and vCenter services that can run in a management cluster:

- Single-Sing-On (SSO)

- Inventory Services

- Web client

- VMware Update Manager (VUM)
- vShield
- Cisco Nexus
- vCenter Operation Manager (VCOPS)
- Third-party software for example anti-virus
- Active Directory for authentication

How to start?

Before we start, we have to ask our self some questions:

1. Do I want a High Available (HA) setup?
2. Do I want to use self singed SSL certificates or do I want to use a PKI environment (public or private)?
3. Witch database do I want to use?
4. Witch type of load balancer do I want to use?

So let us assume that we want to setup a management cluster with the following:

- 2 SSO servers in HA mode on separate virtual machines
- 2 vCenter servers load balanced on separate virtual machines (is this scenario we have to separate vSphere clusters)
- 2 Web clients load balanced on separate virtual machines
- 2 MS SQL database servers in HA mode on separate virtual machines

Some rules that we have to stick to:

- Each vCenter server has his own Inventory Service
- SSO can only be in active/passive mode
- Each vCenter server has his own VUM server.

Design

When we apply these rules we get the following design.

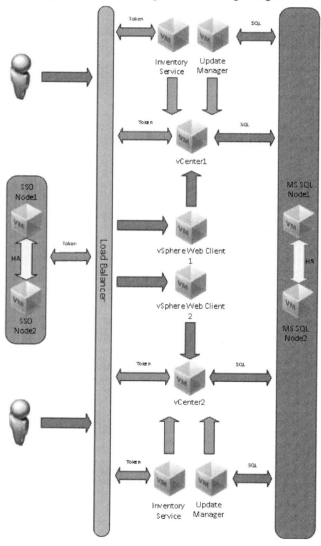

So what do we see here?

Web client

We have two virtual machines running the Web client. These Web clients are behind a load balancer. The load balancer divides the connections equally across the 2 Web client servers. If one Web Client goes down, the other one is still available to manage your VMware environment.

vCenter Server

In this example we have 2 vCenter servers. 1 for a VMware cluster running servers (Exchange, SQL, Etc) and 1 for Horizon View. Nice part is, that both vCenters show up in the same Web Client without linked-mode.

Database

We have 2 Microsoft SQL database servers who are in HA mode with log shipping. This guaranties that if 1 database server goes down, vCenter and other VMware services (Update Manager) for example still continue to work.

VMware Update Manager

Every vCenter Server needs his own Update Manager. This is a one-on-one connection. To prevent that every VUM server has is own patch repository you can share the repository form one VUM server to the other.

Inventory Services

Same, as with VUM, every vCenter server needs his own Inventory server.

So why not place the Inventory Service on the same host a the vCenter server? This way you separate the resources. Inventory is primarily for the Web Client. So to make sure that the Inventory Service doesn't consume resource from the vCenter server we place them on is own hosts.

So why not place them with the Web Clients? What if you get a third vCenter server? Then you have a problem, because this vCenter server also needs a Inventory Service and you only can run 1 Inventory Service per host.

Single Sign-on
Single Sign-on (SSO) came with vSphere 5 and is your central user authentication mechanism. Single Sign-on can have his own user database or makes a connection to (multiple) other authentications services like Microsoft Active Directory. Therefore we don't want only 1 SSO server. If this one fails, nobody can authenticate to vCenter including VUM or other VMware servers as VMware vShield.

SSO can be configured in HA mode, but you have to have a load balancer.

Load Balancer
Most VMware services can be load balanced but they can't do it by themselves. You have to make use of a third-party solution. This can either be a software or a hardware load balancer. Make sure you are aware of the functionality you need. Then pick your load balancer.

Separate or combine services?

In a small deployment you can combine several VMware service on the same virtual machine. But always keep in mind that those services can affect each other in a stress situation, leaving you with a environment you can't manage.

What's missing in this picture?

In this picture we don't see Microsoft Active Directory services for AD authentication or any other third-party software solutions for example anti-virus. If your going to implement a VMware management cluster it's very likely that those services also run in the VMware management cluster.

Conclusion

In a small environment you perfectly can combine multiple VMware services (vCenter, SSO, Inventory and Web client) on the same host.

As you environment grows, more and more services depend on your VMware environment. In case of a complete power-down situation you first want to start your VMware management cluster. This gives you the option to start other service for you production environment controlled.

Make sure before you start you create a solid design. Talk to you customer and stakeholders. Those are the guys paying for it!

About the Author

Michael Wilmsen is a dutch self employed VMware consultant/trainer and founder of the virtualisation website virtual-hike.com. Michael has more than 15 years of experience in IT. Starting as a Novell consultant/trainer he switched to VMware as of ESX 2. Michael has the following certifications VCAP, VCP-DCA, VCAP-DCD, VCAP-DCA, is a vExpert for more than 4 years and is a PernixPro.

You can connect with Michael on Twitter @WilmsenIT

Chapter 3 – Storage Configuration

Thin Provisioning Considerations When Formatting Volumes in a Guest OS

I had this question recently regarding the best way to format volumes in a Windows 2008 Guest OS, and if there were any considerations with the different formatting types on a volume which resides on a thin provisioned VMDK. Just to be certain that what I was stating was actually true, I set up a small test. Bottom line – use quick format when formatting the volume as a normal format will fill the volume, negating the space-saving associated with thin provisioned volumes.

Let's begin by first of all adding a few 10GB thick volumes to this VM, a Windows 2008 Guest OS. As you can see these are 'Thick Provisioned Lazy Zero'.

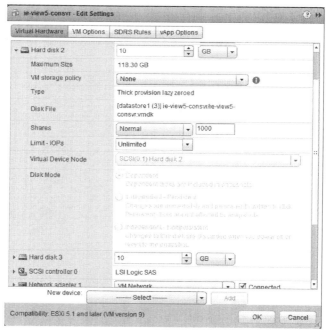

And as expected, when we look via the ESXi host at how much space is consumed on the VMFS volume on which the VMDK resides, we can see that there is indeed 10GB of space consumed by the flat files for these disks. This is before we do anything in the Guest OS.

```
● ○ ○                          chogan — ssh — 107×24
20.0G    .
/vmfs/volumes/5214fb68-6b528b48-2cec-984be10a3212/ie-view5-consvr # ls -al
total 20972552
drwxr-xr-x  1 root    root         840 May 20 10:59 .
drwxr-xr-t  1 root    root        1400 May 20 10:59 ..
-rw-------  1 root    root  10737418240 May 20 10:59 ie-view5-consvr-flat.vmdk
-rw-------  1 root    root         476 May 20 10:59 ie-view5-consvr.vmdk
-rw-------  1 root    root  10737418240 May 20 10:59 ie-view5-consvr_1-flat.vmdk
-rw-------  1 root    root         478 May 20 10:59 ie-view5-consvr_1.vmdk
/vmfs/volumes/5214fb68-6b528b48-2cec-984be10a3212/ie-view5-consvr # ls -al
total 20972552
drwxr-xr-x  1 root    root         840 May 20 10:59 .
drwxr-xr-t  1 root    root        1400 May 20 10:59 ..
-rw-------  1 root    root  10737418240 May 20 10:59 ie-view5-consvr-flat.vmdk
-rw-------  1 root    root         476 May 20 10:59 ie-view5-consvr.vmdk
-rw-------  1 root    root  10737418240 May 20 10:59 ie-view5-consvr_1-flat.vmdk
-rw-------  1 root    root         478 May 20 10:59 ie-view5-consvr_1.vmdk
/vmfs/volumes/5214fb68-6b528b48-2cec-984be10a3212/ie-view5-consvr # du -ah
10.0G    ./ie-view5-consvr-flat.vmdk
0        ./ie-view5-consvr.vmdk
10.0G    ./ie-view5-consvr_1-flat.vmdk
0        ./ie-view5-consvr_1.vmdk
20.0G    .
/vmfs/volumes/5214fb68-6b528b48-2cec-984be10a3212/ie-view5-consvr #
```

OK. So now I will add 2 additional 15GB thin disks to the VM.

And now when I examine the actual space consumed on the VMFS, I see that these flat files are not consuming any space yet.

```
/vmfs/volumes/5214fb68-6b528b48-2cec-984be10a3212/ie-view5-consvr # ls -al
total 20972552
drwxr-xr-x   1 root     root         1400 May 20 11:14 .
drwxr-xr-x   1 root     root         1400 May 20 10:59 ..
-rw-------   1 root     root  10737418240 May 20 10:59 ie-view5-consvr-flat.vmdk
-rw-------   1 root     root          476 May 20 10:59 ie-view5-consvr.vmdk
-rw-------   1 root     root  10737418240 May 20 10:59 ie-view5-consvr_1-flat.vmdk
-rw-------   1 root     root          478 May 20 10:59 ie-view5-consvr_1.vmdk
-rw-------   1 root     root  16106127360 May 20 11:07 ie-view5-consvr_2-flat.vmdk
-rw-------   1 root     root          504 May 20 11:07 ie-view5-consvr_2.vmdk
-rw-------   1 root     root  16106127360 May 20 11:14 ie-view5-consvr_3-flat.vmdk
-rw-------   1 root     root          504 May 20 11:14 ie-view5-consvr_3.vmdk
/vmfs/volumes/5214fb68-6b528b48-2cec-984be10a3212/ie-view5-consvr # du -ah
10.0G   ./ie-view5-consvr-flat.vmdk
0       ./ie-view5-consvr.vmdk
10.0G   ./ie-view5-consvr_1-flat.vmdk
0       ./ie-view5-consvr_1.vmdk
0       ./ie-view5-consvr_2-flat.vmdk
0       ./ie-view5-consvr_2.vmdk
0       ./ie-view5-consvr_3-flat.vmdk
0       ./ie-view5-consvr_3.vmdk
20.0G   .
/vmfs/volumes/5214fb68-6b528b48-2cec-984be10a3212/ie-view5-consvr #
```

Next, let's do some tasks in the Guest OS to make these disks useful. Initially, all 4 disks (both the thick and thin) are offline and are unallocated. The 10GB ones are the thick disks, the 15GB ones are the thin disks.

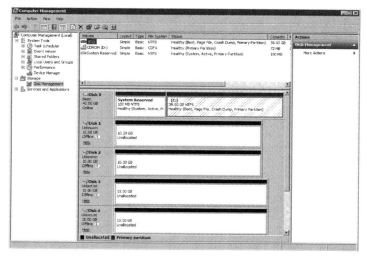

My first step is to bring the volumes online/initialize them. I am only doing this on the thin disks.

After the disks have been initialized (not formatted), I can now see that they have begun to consume some space on the VMFS volume. Since VMFS-5 blocks are allocated in 1MB chunks, one block is needed for initialization.

```
● ○ ○                              chogan — ssh — 107×24
-rw-------    1 root     root           504 May 20 11:07 ie-view5-consvr_2.vmdk
-rw-------    1 root     root     16106127360 May 20 11:14 ie-view5-consvr_3-flat.vmdk
-rw-------    1 root     root           504 May 20 11:14 ie-view5-consvr_3.vmdk
/vmfs/volumes/5214fb68-6b528b48-2cec-984be10a3212/ie-view5-consvr # du -ah
10.0G   ./ie-view5-consvr-flat.vmdk
0       ./ie-view5-consvr.vmdk
10.0G   ./ie-view5-consvr_1-flat.vmdk
0       ./ie-view5-consvr_1.vmdk
0       ./ie-view5-consvr_2-flat.vmdk
0       ./ie-view5-consvr_2.vmdk
0       ./ie-view5-consvr_3-flat.vmdk
0       ./ie-view5-consvr_3.vmdk
20.0G   .
/vmfs/volumes/5214fb68-6b528b48-2cec-984be10a3212/ie-view5-consvr # du -ah
10.0G   ./ie-view5-consvr-flat.vmdk
0       ./ie-view5-consvr.vmdk
10.0G   ./ie-view5-consvr_1-flat.vmdk
0       ./ie-view5-consvr_1.vmdk
1.0M    ./ie-view5-consvr_2-flat.vmdk
0       ./ie-view5-consvr_2.vmdk
1.0M    ./ie-view5-consvr_3-flat.vmdk
0       ./ie-view5-consvr_3.vmdk
20.0G   .
/vmfs/volumes/5214fb68-6b528b48-2cec-984be10a3212/ie-view5-consvr #
```

Now we are ready to actually format the drive. In this first test, I am going to use the 'Quick Format' option to initialize the volume. A quick format is the default, and it is selected automatically. This is basically clearing the table of contents on the drive, and not touching any of the data blocks.

Storage Configuration | 3-5

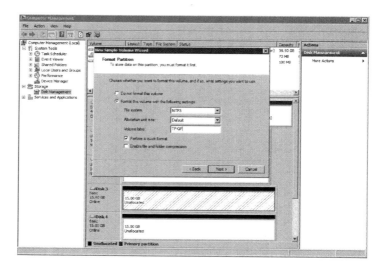

Once the quick format has completed, I return to my ESXi host, and see how much space has been consumed.

```
●○○                    chogan — ssh — 107×24
0        ./ie-view5-consvr_3-flat.vmdk
0        ./ie-view5-consvr_3.vmdk
20.0G    .
/vmfs/volumes/5214fb68-6b528b48-2cec-984be10a3212/ie-view5-consvr # du -ah
10.0G    ./ie-view5-consvr-flat.vmdk
0        ./ie-view5-consvr.vmdk
10.0G    ./ie-view5-consvr_1-flat.vmdk
0        ./ie-view5-consvr_1.vmdk
1.0M     ./ie-view5-consvr_2-flat.vmdk
0        ./ie-view5-consvr_2.vmdk
1.0M     ./ie-view5-consvr_3-flat.vmdk
0        ./ie-view5-consvr_3.vmdk
20.0G    .
/vmfs/volumes/5214fb68-6b528b48-2cec-984be10a3212/ie-view5-consvr # du -ah
10.0G    ./ie-view5-consvr-flat.vmdk
0        ./ie-view5-consvr.vmdk
10.0G    ./ie-view5-consvr_1-flat.vmdk
0        ./ie-view5-consvr_1.vmdk
91.0M    ./ie-view5-consvr_2-flat.vmdk
0        ./ie-view5-consvr_2.vmdk
1.0M     ./ie-view5-consvr_3-flat.vmdk
0        ./ie-view5-consvr_3.vmdk
20.1G    .
/vmfs/volumes/5214fb68-6b528b48-2cec-984be10a3212/ie-view5-consvr #
```

OK. It would appear that only 91MB of the drive that was formatted using the quick format option have been consumed by that operation. So our thin provisioned datastore is still providing some value here. Let's now proceed with formatting my other 15GB volume using a full format option (i.e. uncheck the quick format option)

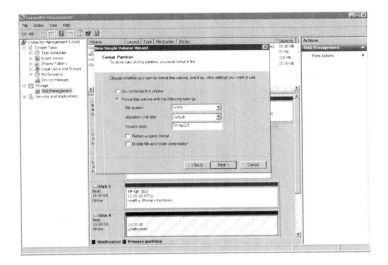

The first thing you will notice is that the formatting takes a lot longer, and is a gradual process. The difference here is that the data blocks are also being zeroed out.

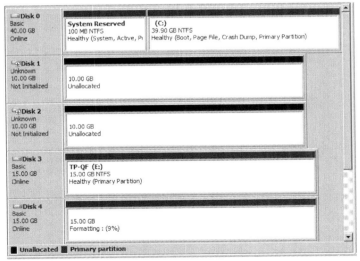

Storage Configuration | 3-7

When this format is complete, I check the amount of space consumed on the VMFS volume once again. Now you can see that the whole of my thin provisioned VMDK is consuming its full amount of allocated space, negating its thin provisioning properties.

```
1.0M    ./ie-view5-consvr_3-flat.vmdk
0       ./ie-view5-consvr_3.vmdk
20.0G   .
/vmfs/volumes/5214fb68-6b528b48-2cec-984be10a3212/ie-view5-consvr # du -ah
10.0G   ./ie-view5-consvr-flat.vmdk
0       ./ie-view5-consvr.vmdk
10.0G   ./ie-view5-consvr_1-flat.vmdk
0       ./ie-view5-consvr_1.vmdk
91.0M   ./ie-view5-consvr_2-flat.vmdk
0       ./ie-view5-consvr_2.vmdk
1.0M    ./ie-view5-consvr_3-flat.vmdk
0       ./ie-view5-consvr_3.vmdk
20.1G   .
/vmfs/volumes/5214fb68-6b528b48-2cec-984be10a3212/ie-view5-consvr # du -ah
10.0G   ./ie-view5-consvr-flat.vmdk
0       ./ie-view5-consvr.vmdk
10.0G   ./ie-view5-consvr_1-flat.vmdk
0       ./ie-view5-consvr_1.vmdk
91.0M   ./ie-view5-consvr_2-flat.vmdk
0       ./ie-view5-consvr_2.vmdk
15.0G   ./ie-view5-consvr_3-flat.vmdk
0       ./ie-view5-consvr_3.vmdk
35.1G   .
/vmfs/volumes/5214fb68-6b528b48-2cec-984be10a3212/ie-view5-consvr #
```

This is the reason why VMware recommends using Quick Format when prepping drives in a Windows Guest OS if you wish to leverage the thin provisioned features of the VMDK. This is also highlighted in KB article 1005418.

About the Author

Cormac Hogan is a Storage Architect in the Integration Engineering team which is part of VMware's vCloud Suite Business Unit. He was one of the first VMware employees at the EMEA headquarters in Cork, Ireland (April 2005) and has previously held roles in VMware's Technical Marketing and Support organizations. He has written a number of storage related white papers and has given numerous presentations on storage best practices and features. He recently co-authored a book entitled "Essential VSAN" with Duncan Epping. He blogs about storage and virtualisation on http://cormachogan.com and you can follow him on twitter via @CormacJHogan.

Host Isolation Response Configuration for IP Storage

Problem Statement

What is the most suitable HA / host isolation response when using IP based storage (iSCSI / NFS)?

Assumptions

1. vSphere 5.0 or greater (To enable use of Datastore Heartbearting)
2. Converged Network used for IP storage is highly available.

Motivation

1. Minimize the chance of a false positive isolation response
2. Ensure in the event the storage is unavailable that virtual machines are promptly shutdown to allow HA to restart VMs on hosts which may not be impacted by IP storage connectivity issues.
3. Minimize impact on the applications/data and downtime.

Architectural Decision

Configure the following:

"das.usedefaultisolationaddress" To "FALSE"

"das.isolationaddress1" : ISCSI/NFS Target 1 e.g: 192.168.1.10

"das.isolationaddress2" : ISCSI/NFS Target 2 e.g: 192.168.2.10

Utilize Datastore heartbeating with multiple datastores (Manually selected or Automatic).

Configure Host Isolation Response to: Power off.

Justification

1. In the event the iSCSI or NFS targets cannot be reached, all datastores will be inaccessible which prevents VMs from functioning normally.

2. If the storage is inaccessible, VMs cannot be "Shutdown" therefore selecting "Power Off" as the isolation response prevents the VM being delayed by the 300 second "Shutdown" time-out before it is powered off, thus improving the achievable recovery time.

3. In the event the isolation response is triggered and the isolation does not impact all hosts within the cluster, the VM will be restarted by HA onto a surviving host without delay.

Implications

1. In the unlikely event the storage connectivity outage is longer than 30 seconds for vSphere 5.0 environments (or 60 seconds for vSphere 5.1 onward) but LESS than the I/O time-out within the Guest (Default 60 Seconds for Windows) the VM will be powered off (Ungracefully shut down) unnecessarily as it could have continued to run without suffering I/O time-outs and the storage would have been restored before the guest OS time-out was issued.

Alternatives

1. Set Host isolation response to "Leave Powered On"

2. Do not use Datastore heartbeating

3. Use the default isolation address

About the Author

Josh Odgers is a virtualization evangelist & industry thought leader who enjoys speaking at industry events & blogging/tweeting. Josh has been awarded the titles of vExpert in 2013/2014 & vChampion (2011/12/13/14) and he is a VMware Certified Design Expert (VCDX). In his role as a Senior Solutions & Performance Engineer at Nutanix, Josh is responsible for performance testing/optimization & developing reference architectures for solutions, mainly focused around Business Critical Applications

Name: Josh Odgers
Twitter: @josh_odgers
Blog: www.joshodgers.com

The Parent Virtual Disk Has Been Modified Since the Child was Created

Some VMs in my environment had virtual-mode RDMs on them, along with multiple nested snapshots. Some of the RDMs were subsequently extended at the storage array level, but the storage team didn't realize there was an active snapshot on the virtual-mode RDMs. This resulted in immediate shutdown of the VMs and a vSphere client error "The parent virtual disk has been modified since the child was created" when attempting to power them back on.

I had done a little bit of work dealing with broken snapshot chains before, but the change in RDM size was outside of my wheelhouse, so we logged a call with VMware support. I learned some very handy debugging techniques from them and thought I'd share that information here. I went back into our test environment and recreated the situation that caused the problem.

In this example screenshot, we have a VM with no snapshot in place and we run vmkfstools –q –v10 against the vmdk file

-q means query, -v10 is verbosity level 10

The command opens up the disk, checks for errors, and reports back to you.

In the second example, I've taken a snapshot of the VM. I'm now passing the snapshot VMDK into the vmkfstools command. You can see the command opening up the snapshot file, then opening up the base disk.

In the third example, I pass it the snapshot vmdk for a virtual-mode RDM on the same VM - it traverses the snapshot chain and also correctly reports that the VMDK is a non-passthrough raw device mapping, which means virtual mode RDM.

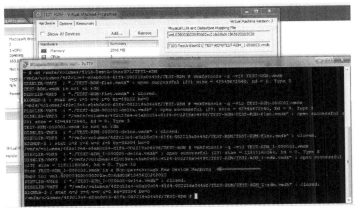

Storage Configuration | 3-13

Part of the problem that happened was the size of the RDM changed (increased size) but the snapshot pointed to the wrong smaller size. However, even without any changes to the storage, a corrupted snapshot chain can happen during an out-of-space situation.

I have intentionally introduced a drive geometry mismatch in my test VM below – note that the value after RW in the snapshot TEST-RDM_1-00003.vmdk is 1 less than the value in the base disk TEST-RDM_1.vmdk

```
/vmfs/volumes/4f2c13e4-e5ab0c54-61f4-0022192449f/TEST-RDM # cat TEST-RDM_1-000003.vmdk
# Disk DescriptorFile
version=1
encoding="UTF-8"
CID=72861eac
parentCID=72861eac
isNativeSnapshot="no"
createType="vmfsSparse"
parentFileNameHint="TEST-RDM_1.vmdk"
# Extent description
RW 23068671 VMFSSPARSE "TEST-RDM_1-000003-delta.vmdk"

# The Disk Data Base
#DDB

/vmfs/volumes/4f2c13e4-e5ab0c54-61f4-0022192449f/TEST-RDM # cat TEST-RDM_1.vmdk
# Disk DescriptorFile
version=1
encoding="UTF-8"
CID=72861eac
parentCID=ffffffff
isNativeSnapshot="no"
createType="vmfsRawDeviceMap"

# Extent description
RW 23068671 VMFSRDM "TEST-RDM_1-rdm.vmdk"

# The Disk Data Base
#DDB

ddb.deletable = "true"
ddb.virtualHWVersion = "7"
ddb.longContentID = "73f15eea9b5e05cc5791bba972961eac"
ddb.uuid = "68 00 C2 98 37 4c 25 8b-8d f2 4a 58 bb 92 1d 67"
```

Now if I run it through the vmkfstools command, it reports the error that we were seeing in the vSphere client in Production when trying to boot the VMs – "The parent virtual disk has been modified since the child was created". But the debugging mode gives you an additional clue that the vSphere client does not give – it says that the capacity of each link is different, and it even gives you the values (20368672 != 23068671).

The fix was to follow the entire chain of snapshots and ensure everything was consistent. Start with the most current snap in the chain. The "parentCID" value must be equal to the "CID" value in the next snapshot in the chain. The next snapshot in the chain is listed in the "parentFileNameHint". So TEST-RDM_1-00003.vmdk is looking for a ParentCID value of 72861eac, and it expects to see that in the file TEST-RDM_1.vmdk.

If you open up Test-RDM_1.vmdk, you see a CID value of 72861eac – this is correct. You also see an RW value of 23068672. Since this file is the base RDM, this is the correct value. The value in the snapshot is incorrect, so you have to go back and change it to match. All snapshots in the chain must match in the same way.

I change the RW value in the snapshot back to match 23068672 – my vmkfstools command succeeds, and I'm also able to delete the snapshot from the vSphere client

About the Author

Patrick Kremer is a Senior Systems Engineer from Chicago, Illinois, and has been working in IT since 1998. He specializes in data center virtualization and holds many related certifications including 4 VMware VCAPs. Patrick blogs at www.patrickkremer.com and can be found on Twitter as @KremerPatrick

Chapter 4 – Network and Security Design

What is Network Virtualization?

Data centers exist for the sole purpose to deploy applications. Applications that automate business processes, serve customers better, enter new markets ... you get the idea. It's all about the Apps.

Server Virtualization

Applications are composed with both Compute and Network resources. It doesn't make sense to have one without the other; a symbiotic relationship. And for the last decade, one half of that relationship (Compute) has been light years ahead of the other (Network). **Compute and Network is a symbiotic relationship lacking any symmetry**.

For example, it's possible to deploy (virtual servers) the Compute of an application within seconds, through powerful automation enabled by software on general purpose hardware — Server Virtualization. The virtual network, on the other hand, is still provisioned manually, on specialized hardware, with keyboards and CLIs. Meanwhile the application deployment drags on for days, weeks, or longer, until the network is finally ready.

Server virtualization also enabled Compute with awesomeness like mobility, snapshots, and push button disaster recovery — to name a few. The network, on the other hand, doesn't have the same capabilities. There is no mobility – the network configuration is anchored to hardware. Snapshots of the application's network architecture is next to impossible because the network configuration state is spread across a multitude of disparate network devices (physical and virtual). And recreating the application's network architecture at a second data center (disaster recovery) is a house of cards (at best), if not impossible, without the same automation, untethered mobility, and snapshots. The Compute portion of the application, with all of its virtualization capabilities, is held back from reaching its full potential, anchored to the non-virtualized network.

Network Virtualization is a solution with products that bring symmetry to the symbiotic relationship of Compute & Network. With network virtualization, the application's virtual Network is provisioned in lock step with virtual Compute, with the same level of speed, automation, and mobility. With compute and network working in symmetry, through Server & Network Virtualization, compute and network are deployed together – rather than one waiting for the other. Applications are fully decoupled, with fully automated provisioning, and truly mobile.

What is Virtualization?

Virtualization is the basic act of **decoupling** an infrastructure service from the physical assets on which that service operates. The service we want to consume (such as Compute, or Network) is not described on, identified by, or strictly associated to any physical asset. Instead, the service is described in a data structure, and exists entirely in a software abstraction layer reproducing the service on any physical resource running the virtualization software. The lifecycle, identity, location, and configuration attributes of the service exists in software with API interfaces, thereby unlocking the full potential of automated provisioning.

The canonical example is Server Virtualization, where the familiar attributes of a physical server are decoupled and reproduced in virtualization software (hypervisor) as vCPU, vRAM, vNIC, etc., and assembled in any arbitrary combination producing a unique virtual server in seconds.

The same type of decoupling and automation enabled by server virtualization is made available to the virtual network with Network Virtualization.

What is the Network?

Virtual machines supporting the application often require network connectivity (switching and routing) to other virtual machines and the outside word (WAN/Internet) with security and load balancing. The first network device virtual machines are attached to is a software virtual switch on the hypervisor. The "network" we want to virtualize is the complete L2-L7 services viewed by the virtual machines, and all of the network configuration state necessary to deploy the application's network architecture (n-tier, etc). The network relevant to the virtual machines is sometimes more specifically referred to as the *virtual network*.

Virtual servers have been fully decoupled from physical servers by server virtualization. The virtual network, on the other hand, has not been fully decoupled from the physical network. Because of this, the configuration necessary to provision an application's virtual network must be carefully engineered across many physical and virtual switches, and L4-L7 service appliances. Despite the best efforts of server virtualization, the *application* is still coupled to hardware.

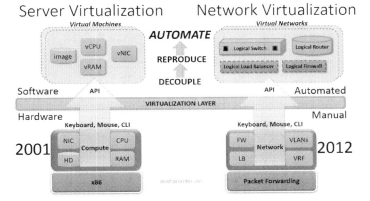

With Network Virtualization, the goal is to take all of the network services, features, and configuration necessary to provision the application's virtual network (VLANs, VRFs, Firewall rules, Load Balancer pools & VIPs, IPAM, Routing, isolation, multi-tenancy, etc.) – take all of those features, decouple it from the physical network, and move it into a virtualization software layer for the express purpose of **automation**.

With the virtual network fully decoupled, the physical network configuration is simplified to provide packet forwarding service from one hypervisor to the next. The implementation details of physical packet forwarding are separated from, and not complicated by, the virtual network. Both the virtual and physical network can evolve independently. The virtual network features and capabilities evolve at software release cycle speeds (months). The physical network packet forwarding evolves at hardware release cycle speeds (years).

Packet forwarding is not the point of friction in provisioning applications. Current generation physical switches do this quite well with dense line-rate 10/40/100G silicon and standard IP protocols (OSPF, BGP). Packet forwarding is not the problem. The problem addressed by network virtualization is the manual deployment of network policy, features, and services constructing the network architecture viewed by application's compute resources (virtual machines).

Network Virtualization

Network Virtualization reproduces the L2-L7 network services necessary to deploy the application's virtual network at the same software virtualization layer hosting the application's virtual machines – the hypervisor kernel and its programmable virtual switch. Similar to how server virtualization reproduces vCPU, vRAM, and vNIC – Network Virtualization software reproduces Logical switches, Logical routers (L2-L3), Logical Load Balancers, Logical Firewalls (L4-L7), and more, assembled in any arbitrary topology, thereby presenting the virtual compute a complete L2-L7 virtual network topology.

All of the feature configuration necessary to provision the application's virtual network can now be provisioned at the software virtual switch layer through APIs. No CLI configuration per application is necessary in the physical network. The physical network provides the common packet forwarding substrate. The programmable software virtual switch layer provides the complete virtual network feature set for each application, with isolation and multi-tenancy.

Server & Network Virtualization

With Network Virtualization the virtual network is entirely provisioned in software, by software, with APIs, at the same speed and agility and in lock step with server virtualization. The same software tools already provisioning the application's virtual machines can simultaneously provision both compute and network together (with templates), and subsequently validate the complete application architecture — compute and network together.

Next, rather than just taking snapshots of virtual machines, take a snapshot of the complete application architecture (compute and network) and ship a copy off to a disaster recovery site – on standby for push button recovery. The application's network is finally equally mobile and running as fast as the compute.

Network Virtualization makes sense because of Server Virtualization. Compute and Network, a symbiotic relationship deployed in synchronization, with symmetry.

It's a no-brainer.

Cheers,
Brad

About the Author

Brad Hedlund is an Engineering Architect with the CTO office of VMware's Networking and Security Business Unit (NSBU), focused on network & security virtualization (NSX) and the software-defined data center. Brad's background in data center networking begins in the mid-1990s with a variety of experience in roles such as IT customer, systems integrator, architecture and technical strategy roles at Cisco and Dell, and speaker at industry conferences. CCIE Emeritus #5530.

Potential Network Black Hole Issue

When I do vSphere and hardware infrastructure health checks very often I meet misconfigured networks usually but not only in blade server environments. That's the reason I've decided to write the article about this issue. The issue is general and should be considered and checked for any vendor solution but because I'm very familiar with DELL products I'll use DELL blade system and I/O modules to show you deeper specifications and configurations

Blade server chassis typically have switch modules as depicted on figure below.

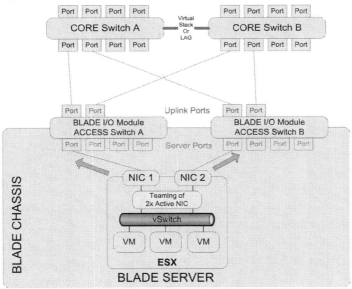

When blade chassis switch modules are connected to another network layer (aggregation or core) then there is possibility of network black hole which I would like to discuss deeply on this post.

Let's assume you will lose single uplink from I/O module A. This situation is depicted below.

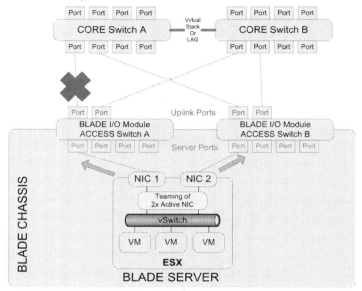

In this situation there is not availability problem because network traffic can flow via second I/O module uplink port. Indeed, there is only half of uplink bandwidth from particular I/O module so there is potential throughput degradation and therefore congestion can occur but everything works and it is not availability issue.

But what happen when second I/O switch module uplink port fails? Look at figure below.

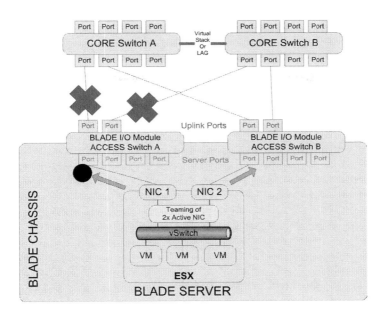

If I/O switch module is in normal switch mode then uplink ports are in link-down state but downlink server ports are in link-up state and therefore ESX host NIC ports are also up and ESX teaming doesn't know that something is wrong down the path and traffic is sending to both NIC uplinks. We call this situation "black hole" because traffic routed via NIC1 will never reach the destination and your infrastructure is in trouble.

To overcome this issue some I/O modules in blade systems can be configured as I/O Aggregator. Some other modules are designed as I/O Aggregators by default and it cannot be changed.

Here are examples of DELL blade switch modules which are switches by default but can be configure to work as I/O Aggregators (aka Simple Switch Mode):

- DELL PowerConnect M6220
- DELL PowerConnect M6348
- DELL PowerConnect M8024-k
- Example of implicit I/O Aggregators are
- DELL Force10 IOA
- CISCO Nexus B22

CISCO Nexus B22 architecture implemented in DELL Blade System actually isn't typical I/O Aggregator but Fabric Extender which is more like link multiplexer virtualizing physical link into more logical links connected to upstream Nexus 5000 or Nexus 7000. Anyway, at the end it can also help you to effectively avoid potential black hole issue.

When you use DELL "simple switch mode/IO aggregator mode" you have limited switch configuration possibilities. For example you can use the module just for L2 and you cannot use advanced features like access control lists (ACLs). That can be reason you would like to leave I/O module in normal switch mode. But even you have I/O modules in normal switch mode you can configure your switch to overcome potential "black hole" issue. Here are examples of DELL blade switches and technologies to overcome this issue:

- DELL PowerConnect M6220 **(Link Dependency)**
- DELL PowerConnect M6348 **(Link Dependency)**
- DELL PowerConnect M8024-k **(Link Dependency)**
- DELL Force10 MXL **(Uplink Failure Detection)**

- CISCO 3130X **(Link State Tracking)**
- CISCO 3130G **(Link State Tracking)**
- CISCO 3032 **(Link State Tracking)**
- CISCO Nexus B22 **(Fabric Extender)**

If you leverage any of technology listed above then link states of I/O module switch uplink ports are synchronized to the configured downlink ports and ESX teaming driver can effectively do ESX uplink high availability. Such situation is depicted in figure below.

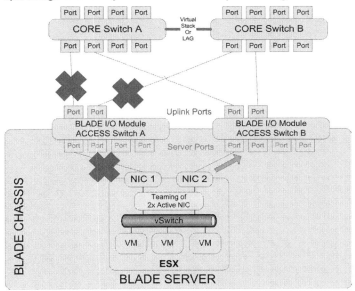

Below are examples of detail CLI configurations of some port tracking technologies described above.

DELL PowerConnect Link Dependency

Link dependency configuration on both blade access switch modules can solve "Network Black Hole" issue.

! Server port configuration
interface Gi1/0/1
switchport mode general
switchport general pvid 201
switchport general allowed vlan add 201
switchport general allowed vlan add 500-999 tagged
! Physical Uplink port configuration
interface Gi1/0/47
channel-group 1 mode auto
exit
! Physical Uplink port configuration
interface Gi1/0/48
channel-group 1 mode auto
exit
! Logical Uplink port configuration (LACP Port Channel)
interface port-channel 1
switchport mode trunk
exit
! Link dependency configuration
link-dependency group 1
add Gi1/0/1-16
epends-on port-channel 1

Force10 Uplink Failure Detection (UFD)

Force 10 calls the link dependency feature UFD and here is configuration example

---

FTOS#show running-config uplink-state-group
!
uplink-state-group 1
no enable
downstream TenGigabitEthernet 0/0
upstream TenGigabitEthernet 0/1
FTOS#

The status of UFD can be displayed by "show configuration" command

---

FTOS(conf-uplink-state-group-16)# show configuration
!
uplink-state-group 16
no enable
description test
downstream disable links all
downstream TengigabitEthernet 0/40
upstream TengigabitEthernet 0/41
upstream Port-channel 8

CISCO Link State Tracking

Link state tracking is a feature available on Cisco switches to manage the link state of downstream ports (ports connected to Servers) based on the status of upstream ports (ports connected to Aggregation/Core switches).

About the Author

David Pasek (VCAP-DCD, VCAD-DCA, vExpert 2014) work for DELL Infrastructure Consulting Services as a Principal Technical Architect focused on data center technologies. David has over 15 years of experience, specialized in Data Center technologies, Servers, Networking, Storage and software automation. He has acted as a Lead Architect in multiple infrastructure projects.

Blog site: http://blog.igics.com

Blog post URL: http://blog.igics.com/2014/04/potential-network-black-hole-issue.html

Twitter: @david_pasek

Enable NIOC (Network I/O Control) on All your Distributed Switches, Wherever Possible

Seems like a no brainer but I am surprised at the number of deployments that do not have it enabled. That is especially true where the network team wants to control bandwidth using its infrastructure in the design phase but then forget to do so once it's all implemented. An important point to consider is that if traffic is controlled outside vSphere, it requires considerable effort to accurately distinguish and control priority for different types of traffic. That is not an issue with NIOC as it understands the different types natively and prioritises accordingly.

I find NIOC to be a great, easy and automated way to police processes that could become bandwidth hogs, when invoked. Some well-known examples are vMotion, creation of pools in VDI environments or cloning in general (where VAAI-compliant storage is not used) and copy operations between datastores etc .

There already are great articles available online, describing how to configure it properly so I won't repeat the process here but my point is to have it enabled, even if in its default state. It is as easy as ticking a box and the default share values are still way better than having no protection at all. The control only kicks in when required and that's ideal as it doesn't affect operations unnecessarily.

Case in point: Recently, I was deploying a floating linked-clone desktop pool using Horizon View 5.3. The process continuously died while cloning the image. The storage being used was iSCSI but not VAAI-compliant.

I noticed that network usage was quite heavy through the various interfaces. However, I also noted the "chaotic" nature of it. All different kinds of traffic were at war with each other. At the time,

I didn't have NIOC enabled on the distributed switch. Looking at that, I decided to enable it and ran the deployment again. This time, it worked without a hitch!

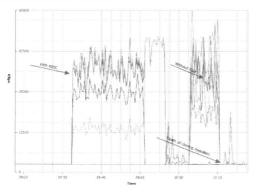

Here, pool deployment with NIOC enabled is on the left and then the same pool deployed without NIOC on the right. As you can see, the traffic on the right looks chaotic and that's what degraded connectivity to the extent that the deployment failed soon after (highlighted by the third arrow). Traffic on the left with NIOC enabled has consistent bandwidth for each type, resulting in solid lines and allows the cloning process to complete successfully.

Another screenshot shows the effect when NIOC is enabled part way through the cloning operation:

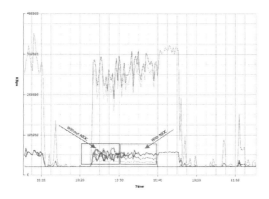

Here again, you can see how enabling NIOC has a positive effect on traffic flow. Initially, NIOC is not enabled so the traffic is irregular and chaotic but enabling it part way, causes all traffic to start taking their fair share on the interfaces, which is consistent and evident from the nice solid lines.

Moral of the story: Enable NIOC on all your distributed switches, wherever possible.

About the Author

Ather Beg has worked in IT professionally for 18 years and became a fan of VMware products when Workstation 1.0 came out. He's a vExpert and his current focus is on everything VMware produces (within reason) and its ecosystem. He is also a PernixPro and honoured to have been featured in v1 of this pocketbook as well.

Blog: http://atherbeg.com

Twitter: @AtherBeg

Designing Redundancy: Designing for Failure

Overview

Virtualization offers many benefits which I will not cover here as you are likely already well aware of many of them as they apply to your environments. The consolidation of servers and hardware can help reduce costs and improve resource utilization. In a physical world this usually means co-locating applications on the same servers but in a virtual environment it is more common to see one application installed per server as servers are much easier and quicker to deploy and this provides isolation between applications making configuration, troubleshooting, and upgrades simpler as there aren't other locally installed business applications to worry about. In either scenario however consolidation does bring a few risks, and somewhat more so in a virtual environment, one of which is that many servers now share a common set of software and hardware and can all be impacted in the case of a problem with any of the underlying and supporting components. This risk can be mitigated however by designing the virtual environment in such a manner as to be able to survive the various failure scenarios that can be foreseen. In other words, by designing for failure.

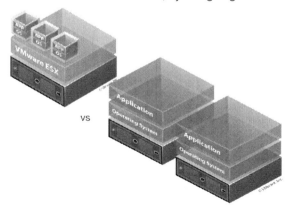

First let's take a look at the basic structure of a virtual environment.

- Host hardware
- Network switches
- Routers
- Storage
- Racks
- Power Distribution
- Data center

We can further break this down into smaller components:

- Host hardware
    - CPU
    - RAM
    - Network interfaces
        - Firmware and drivers
    - Storage adapters
        - Firmware and drivers
    - Power supplies

- Network switches
    - Modules (if not a fixed form factor)
    - ASIC groups
    - Host connections
    - Uplinks
    - Power supplies

- Storage switches (when separate)
    - Host connections
    - Storage array controller connections
    - Power supplies

Storage system
> Storage array controllers
> Power supplies for the controllers
> Power supplies for the disk enclosures

Rack Infrastructure
> Power delivery to the racks (PDUs)

Data center Infrastructure
> Power to the data center
> Cooling

As you can see there are many components and when designing for failure you can take the endeavor as far as you want to go. I will attempt to cover some of the redundancy scenarios in the sections below.

Designing for Networking Redundancy

There are various areas related to networking where we want to have redundancy. On the network infrastructure side, namely the part of the network typically administered by a networking team, we want redundancy for switching and routing. So at a minimum we need to have two switches, each connected to two routers, ideally with multiple connections. This would amount to four pieces of networking equipment. If you choose to use layer 3 switches, that is switches that have both routing and switching capabilities, you can reduce this to two.

This might look like:

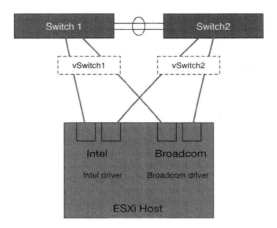

If the storage networking is separate, such as with fiber channel or many iSCSI storage networks, you will want to have a similar setup there with the difference usually being that only storage switches are involved, and they often do not connect to each other in order to maintain completely isolated fabrics, but not always. Consult with your storage vendor for their recommendation based on how they perform failover.

For example:

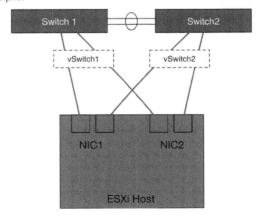

At the virtualization host hardware level we want to provide redundancy for network connectivity as well. If we have network interfaces built into the motherboard, as many servers do, then we also want to have a separate network adapter in the host as well. This allows us to have uplinks to virtual switches from different network adapters. In order to provide networking redundancy at the firmware and driver level we also want to ensure that the networks adapters are of a different make and model and that they use different chipsets. For example one network adapter might be an Intel brand while another one might be Broadcom. Whether they are the same speed is up to you, though I would recommend it for consistency and predictability of performance.

Why would we go to the extent of choosing different adapter brands and chipsets? Well because firmware can have bugs, and drivers can fail, either at the time of install or as they are updated over time as part of the normal life cycle and maintenance operations. By ensuring that drivers and firmware are different on separate networks adapters, and by using separate adapter ports as uplinks to virtual switches, you can ensure that network connectivity is maintained in case of a failure at those levels. Is it likely? I have experienced this at least three times over the years and where I had the host and virtual networking configured as such connectivity was maintained throughout the firmware or driver issue.

I mentioned using different make and model adapter ports as uplinks to virtual switches to provide redundancy to the vSwitch uplinks. This might look like the following:

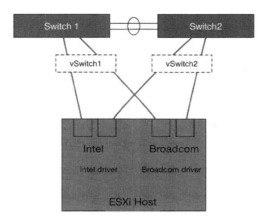

Another item worth looking up and considering is the ASIC to port mapping on your network switches. An ASIC is a chip which is used to make very quick packet handling decision in hardware, essentially a specialized processor. A switch will usually have multiple ASICs with each one being used for a group of ports. The number of ports will vary depending on the vendor and even switch models but knowing what that mapping is can help provide additional resilience to your design.

An example of an ASIC being used to back 6 ports on a switch might be represented as shown in this diagram:

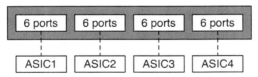

Just like anything else an ASIC can fail. While I have not had it happen often it has happened a handful of times over the years. When an ASIC fails all the ports it backs go with it. Imagine having 6 virtualization hosts each plugged into 6 adjacent switch ports and an ASIC failure causing a loss of connectivity across all 6 hosts at the same time. Spreading your connections across switch port groups on the physical switch can add resiliency. For example if you have 4x 1Gb uplinks from a host going to two switches as 2x 1Gb per switch then connect each cable to a port in a different ASIC on each switch.

This might look like the following:

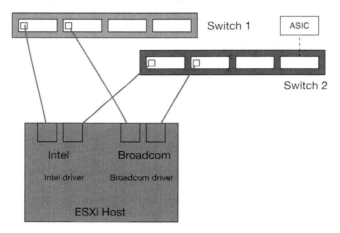

Physical Resilience

Another item to consider is the physical location of your devices whether they be network switches or the hosts themselves. Consolidating hardware into a single rack will save space but comes with potential risk. For example having all of the virtualization hosts in one rack might also mean that two PDUs are shared for all hosts. Spreading them out across multiple racks with multiple PDUs and multiple PDUs upstream in the data center can add resilience. Similarly spreading the switches side by side across two racks might be better than having them in the same rack for the same reason.

Separate racks also protects from physical damage as well. I recall one instance where a contractor doing work on the roof of the building pumped stagnating water into a pipe that we soon found out had not been capped off above the ceiling of the floor below who knows how many years earlier. The result was losing an entire rack of equipment at once as the water fall flowed over the whole rack. Other racks nearby survived the damage.

Wrapping up

Putting all the pieces together the following is what a redundant networking design for a virtual infrastructure might look like. Connectivity and configuration options vary so this is one example. Capabilities such as switch stacking and loop prevention technologies can influence design choices. Detail such as spreading connections across ASICs is not shown but is implied.

Hardware

Server
- Intel dual port 10 Gb network adapter (x2)
- Broadcom dual port 10 Gb network adapter (x2)
- Dual SD cards (for esxi boot)

Server (distribution) switches (x2)
- Storage switches (x2)
- Layer 3 core switches (x2)

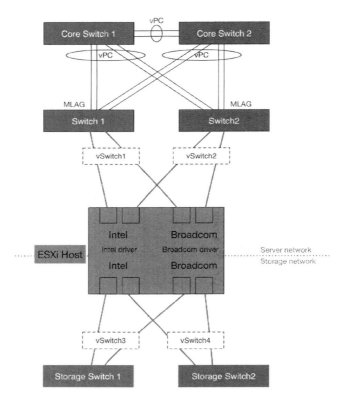

The virtual switches can have the following settings configured for redundancy:

- **Beacon probing** enabled to detect upstream switch or link failures.
- Link-state tracking configured on the upstream switches where supported.
- Multiple vSwitch uplinks using one port from each adapter.
- Multiple uplinks from different physical switches for added redundancy.

Other notes

The core switches might be connected via vPC, or some other virtual switching or stacking capability, so that they present to the downstream switches as a single switch to prevent looping and spanning tree shutting down a path. Each switch closest to the server is uplinked to two separate core switches using multiple links such that one or more connections go to one core switch while the other connections go to the other switch. This ensures connectivity is retained to the downstream switches and to the virtualization hosts in the event of a core switch failure (or one or more links). If you use multiple VDCs (Virtual Device Contexts) then be sure to do this for each VDC.

Summary

As you can see you can take designing redundancy as far as you want to. Budget certainly has an impact when it comes to being able to buy one switch instead or two for example, but there are many other factors to think about such as mixing and matching makes and models (for driver/firmware redundancy for example) and also simpler things such as how uplinks and downlinks are configured. Take some time to really think about any design end to end and plan for failure accordingly. It is much easier to do so when you are putting together requirements versus after you have already begun the purchasing and implementation process - or even after the fact.

About the Author

Peter Chang is a Systems Engineer for PernixData with a background networking, storage, virtualization, and enterprise architecture. He is a two time VMware vExpert and a social media contributor.

Website: virtualbacon.net   Twitter: @virtualbacon

Chapter 5 – VM Configuration

Considerations When Migrating VMs Between vCenter Servers

Something that I really enjoy when I get a chance to, is to speak with our field folks and learn a bit more about our customer environments and some of the challenges they are facing. Last week I had quick call with one of our TAMs (Technical Account Managers) regarding the topic of Virtual Machine migration between vCenter Servers. The process of migrating Virtual Machines between two vCenter Servers is not particularly difficult, you simply disconnect the ESXi hosts from one vCenter Server and re-connect to the new vCenter Server. This is something I have performed on several occasions when I was a customer and with some planning it works effortlessly.

However, there are certain scenarios and configurations when migrating VMs between vCenter Servers that could potentially cause Virtual Machine MAC Address collisions. Before we jump into these scenarios, here is some background. By default, a Virtual Machine MAC Address is automatically generated by vCenter Server and the algorithm is based on vCenter Server's unique ID (0-63) among few other parameters which are documented here. If you have more than one vCenter Server, a best practice is to ensure that these VC IDs are different, especially if they are in the same broadcast domain.

As you can imagine, if you have two vCenter Servers that are configured with the same VC ID, there is a possibility that a duplicate MAC Address could be generated. You might think this is probably a rare event given the 65,000 possible MAC Address combinations. However, it actually happens more frequently than you think, especially in very large scale environments and/or Dev/Test for continuous build/integration environments which I have worked in the past and I have personally seen these issues before.

Going back to our vCenter Server migration topic, there are currently two main scenarios that I see occurring in customer environments and we can explore each in a bit more detail and their implications:

- Migrate ALL Virtual Machines from old vCenter Server to new vCenter Server
- Migrate portion of Virtual Machines from old vCenter Server to new vCenter Server

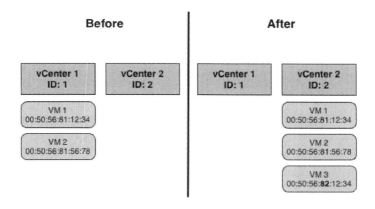

In the diagram above, we have vCenter Server 1 and vCenter Server 2 providing a before/after view. To make things easy, lets say they have VC ID 1 and 2. If we migrate ALL Virtual Machines across, we can see their original MAC Addresses will be preserved as we expect. For any new Virtual Machines being created, the 4th octet of the MAC Address will differ as expected and the vCenter Server will guarantee it is unique. If you want to ensure that new Virtual Machines keep a similar algorithm, you could change the vCenter Server ID to 1. No issues here and the migration is very straight forward.

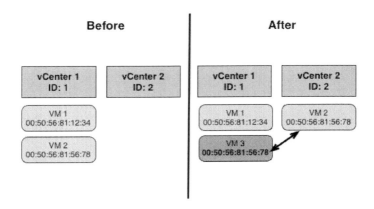

In the second diagram, we still have vCenter Server 1 and vCenter Server with unique VC IDs. However, in this scenario we are only migrating a portion of the Virtual Machines from vCenter Server 1 to vCenter Server 2. By migrating VM2 off of vCenter Server 1, the MAC Address of VM2 is *no longer registered* with that vCenter Server. What this means is that vCenter Server 1 can potentially re-use that MAC Address when it generates a new request. As you can see from the above diagram, this is a concern because VM2 is still using that MAC Address in vCenter Server 2, but vCenter Server 1 is no longer aware of its existence.

The scenario above is what the TAM was seeing at his customer's site and after understanding the challenge, there are a couple of potential solutions:

1. **Range-Based MAC Address allocation** – Allows you to specify a range of MAC Addresses to allocate from which may or may not helpful if the migrated MAC Addresses are truly random

2. **Prefix-Based MAC Address allocation** – Allows you to modify the default VMware OUI (00:50:56) which would then ensure no conflicts would be created with previously assigned

MAC Addresses. Though this could solve the problem, you potentially could run into collisions with other OUI's within your environment

3. **Leave VMs in a disconnected state** — This was actually a solution provided by another TAM on an internal thread which ended up working for his customer. The idea was that instead of disconnecting and removing the ESXi host when migrating a set of Virtual Machines, you would just leave it disconnected in vCenter Server 1. You would still be able to connect the ESXi host and Virtual Machines to vCenter Server 2 but from vCenter Server 1 point of view, the MAC Addresses for those Virtual Machines are seen as in use and it would not be reallocated.

I thought option #3 was a pretty interesting and out of the box solution that the customer came up with. The use case that caused them to see this problem in the first place is due to the way they provision remote environments. The customer has a centralized build environment in which everything is built and then shipped off to the remote sites which is a fairly common practice. Since the centralized vCenter Server is not moving, you can see how previously used MAC Addresses could be re-allocated.

Although option #3 would be the easiest to implement, I am not a fan of seeing so many disconnected systems from an operational perspective as it is hard to tell if there is an issue with the ESXi host and Virtual Machines or because it has been migrated. I guess one way to help with that is to create a Folder called "Migrated" and move all disconnected ESXi hosts into that folder which would help mask that away and disable any alarms for those hosts.

Some additional per-requisite checks that you can perform prior to the partial Virtual Machine migration:

Ensure that the destination vCenter Server is not configured with the same VC ID else you can potentially run into duplicate MAC Address conflicts. You can do this either manually through the vSphere Web/C# Client or leveraging our CLI/API to do so.

Here is an example using PowerCLI to retrieve the vCenter Server ID:

Get-AdvancedSetting -Entity $server -Name instance.id

Ensure no duplicate MAC Addresses exists by comparing the MAC Addresses of the Virtual Machines to be migrated to the Virtual Machines in the new environment. Again, you can either do this by hand (which I would not recommend) or leveraging our CLI/API to extract this information.

Here is an example using PowerCLI to retrieve the MAC Addresses for a Virtual Machine:

Get-VM | Select-Object -Property Name, PowerState, @ {"Name"="MAC";"Expression"={($_ | Get-NetworkAdapter). MacAddress}}

About the Author

William Lam is currently a Staff Engineer working within the VMware R&D organization. He primarily focus on Automation, Integration and Operation of VMware's Software Defined Data center (SDDC). William works closely with various engineering teams within VMware to help provide early feedback on design and architectures. Lastly, through customer interactions and feedback I continue to help champion their challenges and needs to help further improve our products.

VMware vSphere 5.5 Virtual Storage Adapter Performance

A number of you have shown an interest in the relative performance of the different virtual storage adapters that are available in vSphere 5.5. I haven't seen anything published by VMware so I thought I'd do my own testing in my home lab. This is a very brief article to share with you the results I found. Please note: My testing is not real world. I used IOMeter to drive a high amount of IO through a VM for the sole purpose of measuring the relative performance of different adapters under the same conditions. This was not a test to see how fast the VM itself could go, nor what the likely performance might be in a real world scenario. You can't rely on these test results for capacity planning or as a basis of virtualizing one of your applications. Your result may vary and you should verify and validate your own environment and understand your particular application workloads as part of the virtualization process. These results may however assist you when choosing between different virtual storage adapters.

To produce the test results in the image below I used IOMeter on a VM with 2 vCPU and 8GB RAM with different storage adapters and virtual disks connected to each adapter. I used a 100% random read workload and various IO sizes. To keep this article short I've included the data from the 8KB IO size test run. The other tests showed similar relative performance between the different adapters. IOMeter was configured to use a single worker thread and run a different number of outstanding IO's against a single VMDK for each test.

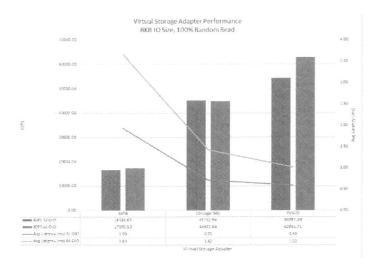

As you can clearly see from the above graph PVSCSI shows the best relative performance with the highest IOPS and lowest latency. It also had the lowest CPU usage. During the 32 OIO test SATA showed 52% CPU utilization vs 45% for LSI Logic SAS and 33% for PVSCSI. For the 64 OIO test CPU utilization stayed relatively the same. If you are planning on using Windows Failover Clustering you are not able to use PVSCSI as LSI Logic SAS is the only adapter supported. Hopefully VMware will allow PVSCSI to be used in cluster configurations in the future.

Final Word

Where possible I recommend using PVSCI. Before choosing PVSCSI please make sure you are on the latest patches. There have been problems with some of the driver version in the past, prior to vSphere 5.0 Update 2. VMware KB 2004578 has the details.

About the Author

Michael Webster is a Senior Solutions and Performance Engineer for Nutanix, VCDX-066, VCAP-CIA, VCAP-CID, vExpert, MCSE, Nutanix Platform Professional. Co-Author of Virtualizing SQL Server on VMware: Doing It Right (VMware Press), Blogger at http://longwhiteclouds.com (top 15 virtualisation blog), on twitter @vcdxnz001, technical reviewer of VCDX Boot Camp and Virtualizing and Tuning Large-Scale Java Platforms, both published by VMware Press. Specializes in solution architecture and performance engineering for Unix to VMware migrations, monster VMs, and virtualizing business critical applications such as Oracle, SAP, SQL, Exchange, Java in software-defined datacenters. More than 20 years in the IT industry and over 10 years experience deploying VMware solutions in large scale environments around the globe. He is regularly presenter at VMware VMworld (Top 10 VMworld Session Speaker 2013), VMware vForums, VMware User Groups and other industry events.

Design considerations for Virtual Machine Time Synchronization

Here are some guidelines and considerations related to time synchronization for your Virtual Machines design. It seems to be a simple topic and covered well online, however I think it deserves better attention as I've seen huge complications in some environments caused by misunderstanding and misconfiguration.

Design Decision

Do not use VMware tools synchronization, instead use guest time synchronization mechanisms.

Justification

Using in-guest timekeeping mechanisms is especially significant for Windows virtual machines which are members of an Active Directory domain because the authentication protocol used by Active Directory, Kerberos, is time sensitive for security reasons. The Windows Domain NTP server should be configured to get its time from an external time source server.

Guests in general should be configured to get their time from AD domain controllers. If not possible then the guests should be configured to use an external NTP source. If this is not practical from a security perspective (exp: you cannot open firewall ports to an external source), then synchronization with host can be an alternative.

Another supporting reason for avoiding VMware tools synchronization is the possible problem caused by excessive CPU overcommitment which can lead to a timekeeping drift at uncorrectable rates by the guests.

Implications

All templates will need to be preconfigured to use an NTP source within the guest OS and the existing VMs will need to be updated to use the same NTP source.

Important Notes

Pay special attention to Domain Controllers and other time sensitive applications, where it is advised to disable time synchronization completely, by adding these lines to the .vmx file of the particular VMs:

---

tools.syncTime = FALSE
time.synchronize.continue = FALSE
time.synchronize.restore = FALSE
time.synchronize.resume.disk = FALSE
time.synchronize.shrink = FALSE
time.synchronize.tools.startup = FALSE

About the Author

Aylin Sali is a virtualization and cloud enthusiast, with 10 years of IT experience. During his past 7 years with IBM he focused on combining virtualization with LEAN thinking Six Sigma techniques for support service improvement. Aylin is a vExpert 2014 and holds several industry certifications such as VMware VCAP5 DCA & DCD, ITIL v3, NetApp NCDA, Microsoft MCITP.

Twitter: @V4Virtual
email: Aylin@thevirtualist.org
Blog: thevirtualist.org

Chapter 6 – Application Landscape

Words of Wisdom...Exchange Virtualization and the Storage Behind It

We all know you can virtualize Exchange; it's supported by Microsoft after all. What seems to still cause unrest, however, is the supported storage architecture for a virtualized Exchange environment, in particular running Exchange on NFS datastores. Now before all the storage vendors that are selling "run Exchange on NFS" jump down my throat, hear me out.

Microsoft's official support statement regarding Exchange storage:

"The storage used by the Exchange guest machine for storage of Exchange data (for example, mailbox databases and transport queues) can be virtual storage of a fixed size (for example, fixed virtual hard disks (VHDs) in a Hyper-V environment), SCSI pass-through storage, or Internet SCSI (iSCSI) storage. Pass-through storage is storage that's configured at the host level and dedicated to one guest machine. All storage used by an Exchange guest machine for storage of Exchange data must be block-level storage because Exchange 2013 doesn't support the use of network attached storage (NAS) volumes, other than in the SMB 3.0 scenario outlined later in this topic. Also, NAS storage that's presented to the guest as block-level storage via the hypervisor isn't supported."- TechNet

What this means is, if you are presenting to your host an NFS datastore and storing the Exchange VMDK's on that datastore, you are running Exchange in a non-supported configuration. Exchange databases — mailbox and transport queues -- are designed to run on block level storage because of how Exchange aborts bad transactions. Since NFS (file level storage) aborts are on a best-effort basis, there is a risk of corruption to the Exchange database.

Given that Exchange storage is ONLY supported on block level storage, it doesn't mean it won't work on an NFS datastore. In fact, with the right storage and enough IOPS, it can run perfectly fine. Microsoft has already said they have no plans to date to invest any time or research into running Exchange on NFS because according to them customers are not asking for it. What this means is that not enough revenue generating customers are asking for Exchange on NFS. Why would Microsoft invest time and research into this when they are pushing Office 365 and all things cloud? Microsoft's focus is cloud first then develop for the On-Premises side of the software. OK, enough of my soapbox and back to words of wisdom.

My words of wisdom for anybody that is considering virtualizing Exchange on NFS:

1. The official support statement from Microsoft is just that, it's about what is supported and not what works and doesn't work, because we know it works. Do your research and reach out to the Exchange Community for any input.

2. The storage vendors should be informing you of what is and is not supported and should stand by their product if they are selling you Exchange on NFS. This means they should be willing to work to the end to resolve any issues that you may encounter. If you can get this in writing, that's even better. I know of a number of storage vendors that will provide you with a written statement of support.

3. Do your research with the storage vendor. Ask for customer references and the size of their deployments. Talk to these references and get their side of the story. Find out their pain points because your storage vendor may not always tell you about them.

Every environment is different with different requirements. Choose the design that best matches your requirements are and start from there. If that means running Exchange on NFS, be sure to get the full support of your storage vendor.

Now that we have this whole NFS thing out of the way, let's talk about some tips for virtualizing Exchange and getting the best performance out of your Exchange VMs. Below is an excerpt from one of my articles on the Petri IT Knowledgebase that highlights some tips and tricks for virtualizing Exchange.

Tips for Virtualizing Exchange

There are probably some administrators that are still concerned about performance issues with running all roles virtualized. It's a valid concern to be sure, but if it's well designed you can have a completely virtualized Exchange environment. For those just getting their feet wet with the idea of virtualizing their Exchange servers, I've made a list of things to look out for to help your transition.

Read the Fine Print

This may seem like a no-brainer, but before you start spinning up VMs, take a glance at Microsoft's support statement for virtualizing Exchange servers. There are also several useful white papers written about virtualizing Exchange. Doing a little research goes a long way to determine the right needs for your particular environment. Here are just a handful:

Microsoft Support Policies and Recommendations for Exchange Servers in Hardware Virtualization Environments

Exchange 2013 Virtualization

Best Practices for Virtualizing Exchange Server 2010 with Windows Server 2008 R2 Hyper V

Understanding Exchange 2010 Virtualization

Virtualizing Exchange with VMware

Split Your Roles

You may want to consider splitting your server roles when you virtualize your Exchange servers. This can improve performance for your Exchange VMs.

Reserve Your Memory

Exchange loves memory, so the more you have, the better. The new versions of Exchange Server have been optimized for performance by using RAM to cache mailbox data. Dynamic memory can have a negative effect on the performance of your Exchange servers by not having enough RAM to cache your data. Slow performing Exchange server means unhappy users.

Turn off DRS or Live Migration

Yep, you read that correctly. Host-based failover is only supported for Exchange VMs if the server is coming up from a cold boot. While you can perform a vMotion of your Exchange server, it is not supported to do so while the server is powered on. If you are running VMware, you can modify the VMs settings to prevent any DRS actions. If you're running a DAG, you don't need vMotion because your passive databases on another VM will handle the high availability of the mailboxes.

Know Your Storage

Exchange does not support NFS for Exchange data. Storage presented to an Exchange VM must be block level storage. NFS is a common protocol used in a lot of VMware environments; if you are in one of them, you will need to look at other protocols to present the storage to yours VMs. The ideal way of presenting storage to an Exchange VM is to use pass-through storage from the host to the

VM. Software iSCSI inside the guest VM is also supported, but there are performance considerations you must account for.

No Snapshots

Snapshots are a way the Hypervisor allows you to capture the state of a VM at a particular moment while it's running, giving you an opportunity to revert back to it at a later time. Snapshots are great but they are not application aware, which could cause issues if a server were to revert back to an older snapshot. Performing snapshots on an Exchange VM is not supported. Yes, you can still do it. There is nothing stopping you from clicking that button, but it's just best to step away from the snapshot button. If you're running a lab it may not be a big issue, but on a production server I would avoid doing snapshots of the VMs.

Only Use SATA Disks Under Certain Conditions

The use of lower-cost storage such as SATA disks is very enticing, especially as the need for more mailbox storage grows. But wait! Before you jump on the SATA bandwagon, do the research to determine whether SATA drives will give you enough IOPS to support your environment. You may find that it is more cost effective to run the data on faster drives rather than buying a 100 SATA drives to give you enough spindles for your IOPS.

Unified Messaging has Limited Virtualization Support

The unified messaging role is only supported in a VM for Exchange 2010 SP1 or later. You will need to upgrade to a new version if you are running anything older than that.

These are just a few items to consider when virtualizing your Exchange servers that can help with your design. Virtualizing all your Exchange servers is definitely possible and can even reduce hardware costs. I have personal experience running a completely virtualized Exchange environment for a large enterprise, so I know it can be done — and it runs great. Using virtualization to run an

Exchange environment can reduce your hardware footprint as well as allowing you to utilize more of your investment in your virtualization environment.

About the Author

Phoummala Schmitt is a Sr Systems Engineer with a broad range of experiences from supporting the SMB market to a Global Enterprise. Her specialties include Microsoft Exchange Server, VMware, and various Storage and Enterprise Backup technologies. In her spare time she writes for the Petri IT Knowledgebase and The Register.

Twitter: @exchangegoddess

Blog: exchangegoddess.com

Impact of Write Acceleration on Your Backups

As an architect focused on storage and virtualization solutions, I commonly find myself in conversations with customers who either have or are strongly considering adopting host-based acceleration solutions. As they begin to see the impact these solutions can have on their workloads, we move rather quickly to the question of the larger impact of injecting this kind of a solution into their environment. This conversation is all the more important if the host-based solution offers, and the customer will leverage, write acceleration.

Impact of Write Back

When you accelerate both reads and writes at the host, there are at least two major areas of your data protection strategy that must be updated. First, your array-based replication and second, your VM-level backups. The focus of this article will be on the latter.

VM-level backups are impacted by write-back acceleration as follows: In write-back mode, VM's receive their acknowledgements for new writes from the flash/server tier, and not the storage backing it. So then, at any given point in the operation of the VM, you will have a synchronous zone (VMs and Hosts) and an asynchronous zone (Storage) with regard to application and crash-consistency which is critical to backup and recovery operations. To depict this scenario, consider the following diagram:

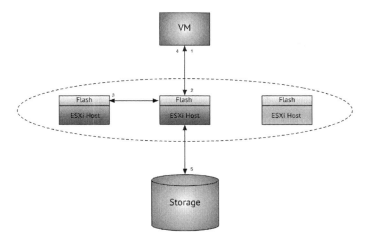

Virtual Workloads in Write-Back Mode

In this diagram, we see the VM sends a write IO to the host (1), the acceleration software writes this IO to local flash (2), and additionally a parity write within the cluster for recoverability (3). At this point, the VM receives an acknowledgment of the write (4) and continues on its way. After the VM has continued with read/write operations, and at a certain interval, the flash acceleration tier will destage this write IO, and others, to the underlying storage (5). This, from the VMs perspective, happens asynchronously and creates the two zones mentioned above.

As a result of this, we need to implement a strategy to provide synchronization between the host and underlying storage during your organization's backup window to ensure we have at minimum a crash-consistent backup of your workload, and hopefully an application consistent one.

Write Back and Backups: Solution

One common method for meeting the above requirement is to transition the VMs from writeback to write-through mode on a programmatic, scheduled basis. In write-through, the acknowledgment back to the host happens only after the underlying storage receives, commits, and acknowledges back to the acceleration tier the write IO as depicted here:

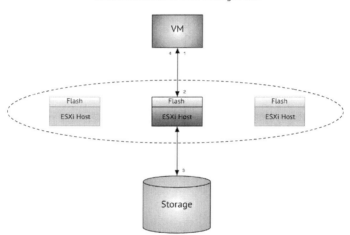

Virtual Workloads in Write-Through Mode

How you will perform this transition will be in large measure down to the platforms you have in place for your host acceleration and backup infrastructure. Often, this will involve some sort of scripting where you will transition the VM pre-backup to write-through, and then return the VM to write-back upon completion of the necessary backup tasks. The period of time the VM is not accelerating writes will be determined by how long the backup solution needs the VM in the write-through state to capture a consistent state of the VM for recovery.

As this will usually happen during a backup window defined by the organization, the impact to production workloads will be minimized while achieving the appropriate levels of data protection and recoverability.

About the Author

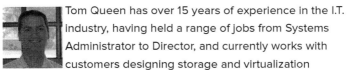

Tom Queen has over 15 years of experience in the I.T. industry, having held a range of jobs from Systems Administrator to Director, and currently works with customers designing storage and virtualization solutions. For his work, he has been recognized as a VMware vExpert, and holds certifications from VMware and EMC. He blogs at http://www.tracinglines.net and tweets @linetracer.

Chapter 7 – Words of Wisdom

vSphere Web Client Short Cuts

Every once in a while, you learn about something that is kind of neat. In some conversations with our UI team, I recently learned about a few cool vSphere Web Client short cuts to jump to between different views.

Ctrl + Alt + 1 = Go to Home View

Ctrl + Alt + 2 = Go to vCenter Home View

Ctrl + Alt + 3 = Go to the Hosts & Clusters View

Ctrl + Alt + 4 = Got to the VM & Templates View

Ctrl + Alt + 5 = Got to the Datastores View

Ctrl + Alt + 6 = Go to the Networks View

Ctrl + Alt + S = Place cursor in the Search field

Pretty nice.

About the Author

Cormac Hogan is a Storage Architect in the Integration Engineering team which is part of VMware's vCloud Suite Business Unit. He was one of the first VMware employees at the EMEA headquarters in Cork, Ireland (April 2005) and has previously held roles in VMware's Technical Marketing and Support organizations. He have written a number of storage related white papers and has given numerous presentations on storage best practices and features. He recently co-authored a book entitled "Essential VSAN" with Duncan Epping. He blogs about storage and virtualisation on http://cormachogan.com and you can follow him on twitter via @CormacJHogan.

Systems Thinking Impacting Design Decisions

As with most design decisions it becomes imperative that all steps are taken to prove out a design that meets and exceeds all expected goals. In the world of virtualization, the choices we make are the new foundations of the enterprise. This is why it's more important to get the process right in making a good design decision. It's much easier to correct the implementation than having to go back and start over with the entire process. It is with this mantra that I want to explore one idea on how to implement a Systems Thinking approach for good design decisions in virtualization.

As technologists we thrive on new products and services that tickle our inner ego. This is where it becomes imperative to implement a process that incorporates all inputs that can help drive a successful design decision. The old military adage of "7 P's" (Proper Planning and Preparation Prevents Piss Poor Performance) can even be relevant in a virtualization type of project design. This preparation and planning can be realized in the collection of inputs to a project design, where they can be broken down into smaller pieces for ample analysis. This is called the **Feedback loop** – a causal path that leads from the discovery of a design gap to the subsequent modifications of the design gap.

It's this reciprocal nature of Systems Thinking that provides a constant feedback loop to the design. The ultimate goal is a design that changes based on external parameters to meet a new set of goals or challenges. If you can get to a design like this, then you can become more agile and not have to implement patch solutions to accomplish a new forced or unforeseen change.

To illustrate how such a process can impact design decisions, let's first look at a common problem in many environments. Many organizations are growing their virtualization environment at a rapid pace therefore, there is a constant pressure to provide enough storage capacity/performance as the VMware environment constricts.

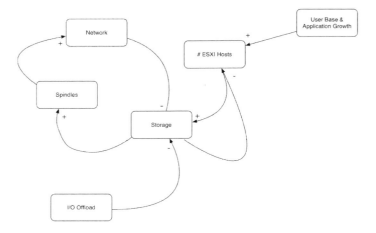

As you can see this is a simple, yet applicable example of a feedback loop that can help you break apart the pieces of a design to come up with an effective solution. Let's now go through the pieces to understand the relationships and the effect they can have on the design.

As the "User Base" or as "Applications" are virtualized this puts added pressure to increase the number of ESXi hosts to support the compute requirements. As in most environments the number of ESXi hosts increase; this will increase the demand and contention on the storage systems to keep up with the I/O load. In order to keep up the capacity growth demands and I/O performance load, this pushes the admin to add more spindles to the storage environment. More spindles allow for more I/O processing which as a result could increase the demand for a faster storage fabric. This loop finally decreases the demand on the storage system in a response to the growth, but as you can see it's only temporary, since there is still added pressure from new user and virtualization growth. The only way to turn the tide on the storage pressure is to instrument a negative reinforcing loop. An "I/O Offload" solution can help by decreasing the demand on the storage system and thus provide better consolidation back onto the ESXi Hosts.

What this illustrates is how a Systems Thinking approach can help overcome some of the complexity in a design decision. This is only a small subset of the possibilities so my intention is to provide more examples of this on my blog. If you want to learn more about Systems Thinking check this short overview to a larger context.
http://www.thinking.net/Systems_Thinking/OverviewSTarticle.pdf

About the Author

Todd Mace is a Systems Engineer for PernixData. He also served in the past as an Information Systems Director for a large non-profit organization. Additionally, he was a Microsoft trainer for a nationally recognized university and a consultant to a large airport authority and nationally recognized auto parts chain. His current certifications include: MCSE, MCT, VCP5 and he is also recognized as a VMware vExpert for 2013 and 2014.

Blog: Cloudjock.com
Twitter: @mctodd

IT Infrastructure Design

Introduction

"All things are created twice" is one of the principles that immediately comes to mind when thinking of designing IT infrastructures. It's the principle by Stephen Covey that says that we first create things in our mind, before we even produce anything in the physical world.

Think about that for a second. We think first before we do something. It's the process we do unconsciously all day long. We do it every moment of the day, over and over again. The same goes for designing new IT infrastructures. First think about it, write that down into design documents and then build the IT infrastructure as defined in your design documents.

Compare it to building a house. Nobody goes out, buys bricks and mortar and then starts building something without a design and a plan. The same goes for building a new IT infrastructure or whatever it is that needs to be thought out before it is created. You don't go out and randomly install software hoping it will result in the optimal IT infrastructure that suits your needs. Or better yet the needs of your customer / company. Cause most of the times you don't design according to what you think is best. You design the infrastructure to suit the needs and requirements of somebody else.

Just like with building a house, you are the architect. Trying to figure out those needs and requirement of your customer. How big it must be? How many people are going to live in it? How should the plumbing / electricity be installed? And last but not least how much in the total amount of money that can be spend?

But we're not building a house; we are building an IT infrastructure. The variables change, but the design methodology is the same. First think of what you want to create, then go out and build it.

Business & IT Infrastructure

Before going into the details on how the IT infrastructure design methodology looks like, one needs to take a step back and look at the bigger picture: Why do we need an IT infrastructure? It may sound like a stupid question, but sometimes it is useful to see look at things from a high level perspective.

The business uses IT to accommodate the delivery of services and / or products to the outside world. Over the years business processes have become more and more reliant on IT services. IT services now a days are the backbone of most business processes and if the IT services fail, the business fails to deliver its services and / or products. So IT has become a crucial part in the way we do business. No matter what business you are in, there is always some form IT service needed to be able to conduct business.

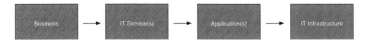

IT services consists out of one or more application stacks. Application stacks by themselves are build up out of one or more servers that host the applications. Those servers need to be hosted and connected through IT infrastructure. It is IT infrastructure that delivers the resources for the applications to run.

So in essence the IT infrastructure is the foundation for hosting the application landscape within companies that is needed to provide IT services. And as already stated IT services are needed to conduct business.

The availability, performance and security of the IT infrastructure are essentials for delivering optimal IT services to the business. A good and solid IT infrastructure starts with a design that takes all these things into account. That's where the IT infrastructure design methodology comes into play with a "first think, then act" mentality.

IT Design Methodology

To be able to create a good design you need to have all the stakeholders involved. Stakeholders are everybody that either works with or depends on the IT infrastructure and is impacted by the decisions made during the IT design process.

Typical roles that we need to look for as stakeholders can be found in the following IT infrastructure areas:

- IT Architecture infrastructure / application / enterprise
- Security
- Application development / management
- Infrastructure Operations
- Project; business / IT

The amount of stakeholders will depend on the company size and the amount of people that actually need to be involved. Sometimes not all topics are relevant as input for the IT design process and sometime people fulfill multiple roles. The stakeholder groups needs to be a good representation in order to get all the requirements for the new infrastructure. To few is not going to be representable for a good design, but to much is going to make the design process sluggish and slow. Most of the times you'll discuss the amount of people with the person handing out the IT design order. They know who should be involved and to what extend.

These people will then be involved in the IT infrastructure design process. Below is a graphical representation of the IT design methodology.

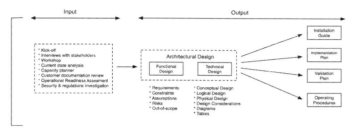

The core of the whole design process is the architectural design. The architectural design is the document that defines the why, how and what of the to-be IT infrastructure. It is the write-up of the think process around IT infrastructure design; the blueprint that will be used for building the IT infrastructure.

The architectural design has two parts: the functional design and the technical design. The two will be explained in depth in the following chapters.

Functional design

The functional design describes what the new IT infrastructure must look like. The input for the functional design comes from the various input methods that an architect can do in order to get the information from the stakeholders.

- **Kick-off meeting**; Every design process should start with kick-off meeting. This meeting involves all the IT infrastructure pre-defined stakeholders. During the meeting the purpose and goals of the design creation will be explained to everyone involved. This will make sure that everybody knows that is going to happen and will help with buy-in into the design process.
- **Interviews with stakeholders**; All stakeholders should be interviews to get their input into the design process. Stakeholders will provide the input to the architect who will document them into the functional design.
- **Workshops**; Workshops can also be beneficial in gathering the input for the functional design. In the workshops the architect and stakeholders will make decisions about design topics and will be documented in the functional design.
- **Current state analysis**; The analysis of the current state can give a good overview of what the current IT infrastructure looks like. This can then be translated into requirements that go into the functional design or can raise design topics that can be addressed in workshops and/or interviews.
- **Customer documentation review**; Documentation about the current IT infrastructure contains information that can be valuable about for the new IT infrastructure design. Review of the current documentation is therefor needed to gather information
- **Operational Readiness Assessment**; An assessment of the current operation can deliver valuable insight into the IT organization and generate requirements and / or constraints for the new IT infrastructure design. Technically everything is possible, but people and process also needs to be taken into account when designing the new IT infrastructure.

- **Security & regulations investigations**; Depending on the business it is useful investigate security and regulations requirements. This makes sure that the IT infrastructure meets the standards defined by security or regulations defined by local law.

All the input will be gathered into the functional design. The functional design is the definition of how the new IT infrastructure should look like. Look at it as an agreement between the stakeholders and the people responsible of designing and building the new infrastructure. It is therefor recommended to review, validate and sign-off the functional design with the sponsor and stakeholders before continuing with the technical design.

After all you first want to have a clear understanding of what needs to be created before continuing with the technical bits and pieces. The formal sign-off of the functional design creates and agreement between both parties. If during the technical design or implementation discussion arise about what needs to be created, one can turn back to the functional design to look up and see what was agreed upon upfront. It creates clarity for the architect on what needs to be created and for the sponsor and stakeholder on what they are actually are going to get in the end.

Therefore good functional design has to be clear and understandable for all parties involved. The following aspects should be written down into a functional design document:

Requirements

Requirements are the definition of what the new IT infrastructure should look like. Each requirement is part of the definition of the new IT infrastructure. Requirements are gathered from the stakeholders through the various input methods. The requirements can be categorized for IT infrastructure in the following design areas:

- Manageability
- Availability
- Performance
- Recoverability
- Security

Examples of requirements are:

- "The availability level defined for the IT infrastructure is 99,99%"
- "Role Based Access Control (RBAC) needs to be implemented in the IT infrastructure."

Constraints/Givens

Some facts are already defined upfront or design decisions have already been made before the design process took place. These are things that can not be changed and are no longer under the influence of the IT infrastructure design team. These facts are defined as constraints and / or givens in the functional design.

Examples of constraints / givens are:

- "Customer has bought Compute rack servers of type XLarge 1024. These servers need to be used in the IT infrastructure"
- "The IT infrastructure needs to be located in the customers two datacenters in A and B."

Assumptions

One needs to make a assumption if input for the technical design is needed, but isn't available at the time of defining the functional design. The assumption will be defined by the stakeholders and the architect, as been the most probable fact. All assumptions are documented into the functional design.

Examples of assumptions are:

- "The available hardware provides enough resources to host 1000 virtual machines."
- "Users, specifically with administrator privileges, have sufficient knowledge of IT infrastructure products to be able to manage the IT infrastructure accordingly."

Out-of-Scope

Things that are not part of the new IT infrastructure design will be defined as out-of-scope. Not everything needs to be listed of course, but if the assumption could arise if something is part of the design, but isn't, then list it under out-of-scope to be sure. This will define clearly where the scope is of the design process.

Examples of out-of-scope definitions are:

- "The re-design of the VDI environment is out-of-scope of this design process."
- "Disaster recovery of the IT infrastructure will not be defined during the design process."

Risks
Risks are facts that are not under the influence of the IT Infrastructure design team, but do impact the IT infrastructure design. Every identified risk needs to be written down and documented in the functional and / or technical design. Preferably the risk needs to be documented with a definition how to mitigate the risk. This defines how the risk will be controlled and how the impact on the IT infrastructure design process will be minimized.

Examples of risks are:

- "The server hardware needs for the build of the IT infrastructure will be delivered two weeks before the build takes place."
- "The stakeholders do not have enough time to participate in the design process. This could potentially lead to an incomplete functional design or an extension of the IT infrastructure design project timelines."

All these aspects are defined in the functional design. They define how the stakeholders want the new IT infrastructure to look like. With a complete and signed functional design a start can be made with the technical design.

Technical Design

The technical design is the technical translation of the functional requirements. It defines how the IT infrastructure should be build with the available soft- and hardware. This has to be done while taking the requirements and constraints into account.

High-Level Design
It is useful to make a translation between the functional design and the technical design. The high level design is that translation and provides a conceptual design of the IT infrastructure. This conceptual design will be defined further in depth in the rest of

the technical design. The conceptual design, when finished, is the bridge between the functional design and the technical design.

Data center Design

From the conceptual design a data center design can be derived. This defines how the IT infrastructure resources will be distributed across the data center locations. This defines at a high level how compute, storage and network will be located. Also the definition of the management tooling will be defined in this chapter. It will provide an overview how the resources will be used within the data center and how they will be managed.

Compute Design

Compute defines how processor and memory resources are used. It describes the technical details of the compute setup and how they should be configured and installed. The technical design of the compute layer will define how this will be setup in the data center.

Network Design

All resources need to be connected. For this the network design is created. It defines how infrastructure components communicate with one another and how network traffic flows within the data center. The chapter defines how the network components are connected and how the logical networks are defined within the data center topology.

Storage Design

Storing the data of the IT infrastructure components is crucial. Within data center shared storage is used to store the data of applications and infrastructure components. The technical storage design defines the setup and configuration of the storage components. This needs to be in line with the requirements and constraints in the functional design.

Availability/Recoverability Design
The IT infrastructure needs to provide the availability as defined by the stakeholder. The technical design needs to provide the details how the availability is guaranteed and how availability is achieved in case of IT infrastructure failures. Part of availability is also the recoverability of the IT infrastructure and how the IT infrastructure can be recovered in case of a disaster.

Security Design
Security is one of the design topics that always comes back when designing an IT infrastructure. The technical design needs to provide the configuration to adhere to the security requirements that have been defined in the functional design.

These topics will all be defined in the technical design. The technical design is the technical blueprint how the IT infrastructure will be set up and configured. The technical design results in fulfilling the requirements as defined by the stakeholders in the functional design. This has to be done while taking the constraints and assumptions into account. Only then will the IT infrastructure be build according to the wishes and needs of the stakeholders that use or are depended on the IT infrastructure.

Operational Documentation

Besides the architectural design, with the functional and technical design documentation, the design process also needs to provide guidance on how to implement the technical design within the IT infrastructure. Creating the following documents does this:

Installation Guides
The installation guides are derived from the technical design. They provide in depth detail how to install and configure the components that build up the IT infrastructure. These are step-by-step guides on

every step of the installation and configuration. Part of the installation guides is the workbook with all the install parameters.

Implementation Guide

The implementation guide is the plan that defines in which order and by whom the installation and configuration needs to take place. This makes sure that the IT infrastructure components are installed in the correct order and that every IT infrastructure team knows what to do when and how.

Validation Plan

When all components are installed and configured the IT infrastructure needs to be tested to validate that is has been setup as defined in the functional and technical design. This provided the sign-off and completion of the design process. After successful completion of validation plan the design process is finished and the stakeholder have an IT infrastructure that meets their requirements.

Operational Procedures

The operational procedures are the manual that comes with the new IT infrastructure. It provides the procedures to operate the IT infrastructure and defines the procedures for IT infrastructure management. This will be provided to the IT Infrastructure operations team who are responsible for the day-to-day management of the IT infrastructure.

To Conclude...

Hopefully this IT design methodology has provided some insight on how to design, build and operate an IT infrastructure. Every IT infrastructure is different as it is designed and build based on the requirements and constraints that are provided by the sponsor and stakeholder in the IT infrastructure design process. However the IT Infrastructure design methodology is the same for every design. Following the steps in the IT infrastructure design process will guarantee that the IT infrastructure will be designed and build according to the requirements and specifications defined up front and taking the constraints into considerations.

Only then we can ensure the best IT infrastructure design. "Think first, act second" and everything will end with the best design that fulfills the requirements while taking the constraints into account. IT infrastructure design at its best!

About the Author

Martijn Baecke is a Solutions Consultant at VMware. He is focused on consulting VMware solutions to customers. Martijn is a VMware Certified Design eXpert (VCDX #103) and is a vExpert . He has been working in IT for the last 10+ years and has a Bachelors degree in Computer Science and a Post-Bachelor in Business Management.

Blog : http://thinkcloud.nl

Twitter : @baecke

Made in the USA
Charleston, SC
02 October 2014